the **Healing Power** *of a* **Christian Mind**

Books by Dr. Backus

Finding the Freedom of Self-Control
The Good News About Worry
The Healing Power of a Christian Mind
The Hidden Rift With God
Learning to Tell Myself the Truth
Taking Charge of Your Emotions
   (Audio tape)
Teaching Your Children to Tell Themselves the Truth
   (with Candace Backus)
Telling Each Other the Truth
Telling the Truth to Troubled People
Telling Yourself the Truth (with Marie Chapian)
Telling Yourself the Truth Study Guide
   (with Marie Chapian)
Untwisting Twisted Relationships
   (with Candace Backus)
What Did I Do Wrong? What Can I Do Now?
   (with Candace Backus)

the Healing Power of a Christian Mind

HOW BIBLICAL TRUTH CAN KEEP YOU HEALTHY

Dr. WILLIAM BACKUS

BETHANY HOUSE PUBLISHERS
MINNEAPOLIS, MINNESOTA 55438

Published by Bethany House Publishers
A Ministry of Bethany Fellowship International
11300 Hampshire Avenue South
Minneapolis, Minnesota 55438

Printed in the United States of America by
Bethany Press International, Minneapolis, Minnesota 55438

Library of Congress Cataloging-in-Publication Data

Backus, William D.
    The healing power of a Christian mind : how truth strengthens your immune system / William Backus.
        p.   cm.
    Includes bibliographical references.
    ISBN 0–7642–2101–9 (pbk.)
        1. Health—Religious aspects—Christianity.
2. Psychoneuroimmunology. I. Title.
BT732.B3255   1996
261.8'321—dc20   95–45079
                                                        CIP

To my mother

WILLIAM BACKUS, Ph.D., is a Christian psychologist, an ordained Lutheran clergyman, and the bestselling author of a dozen books, including *Telling Yourself the Truth*. He is founder and director of the Center for Christian Psychological Services in St. Paul, Minnesota. He and his wife, Candace, make their home in Minnesota.

Contents

Sentenced to . . . Life!

Once in a while an unexpected event leaps serendipitously into your life and points you in a new direction. Not long ago I received a letter from a man I'd never met—Dr. Daniel Fountain, a physician in Zaire. Reading about Dr. Fountain's amazing discovery was, for me, one of those exhilarating events.

After introducing himself, Fountain launched into a description of a new AIDS-treatment program which he oversees at the Vanga Hospital in Kinshasa, Zaire. He explained that the AIDS epidemic has ravaged some African countries, including Zaire, where doctors often do not have AZT and other AIDS medications at their disposal. The situation is bleak indeed. But Dr. Fountain, a man of faith, had a hunch. Since he lacked the resources to medicate his patients, he wondered if he could help them treat themselves in another way—that is, by replacing the negative and depressing mind-set that can accompany illness with life-giving spiritual truths.

That caught my attention.

As a clinical psychologist and pastor, I've been well aware for decades how dark depressive thoughts and negative self-talk creates more emotional problems than the actual events that trigger our emotions. *Self-talk* refers to the way we mentally process events—that is, how we interpret things that happen to us. For instance, three men may walk to the store in a snowstorm, slip on the same patch of ice, and experience a minor injury. One may make a neutral observation: "The sidewalks are in worse condition than I thought. I'll be a little more careful." The second may abuse himself with negative and punishing thoughts like, "Why was I so stupid to come out in this bad weather? I hope nobody saw me fall. I feel like such an idiot whenever I goof up." And the third may turn the fall into an opportunity to imagine the worst: "Man, this bruise hurts. I've probably injured myself for life. Better get home and call my chiropractor right away. I'm sure I've done serious nerve damage to myself."

Obviously, three different people could experience different injuries in the same type of fall—but my point is to examine the *self-talk*. The first man used the experience to reinterpret the *weather conditions*; the second man reinterpreted *himself*; the third man reinterpreted the *state of his physical well-being*.

In this same way, each one of us reinterprets actual events—that is, we *color* events—by telling ourselves what to think about them. Can you see how powerful *self-talk* is? That's why it's important to understand how our self-talk—those statements we make to ourselves—form our emotions: powerful feelings like fear, anger, worry. In a very real sense these emotions are only the visible storm clouds created by a whole climate system that's at work within each one of us. And on the other hand, I've observed how countless clients learn to create an internal climate of peace and happiness—a bright, positive-spirited approach to life—no matter what their circumstances might be. And I've observed that this inner climate—this positive approach to life—actually contributes to swifter healing from the emotional punches life throws at them.

But can the mind create an inner climate of well-being that has *physical benefits*? Enough to counter the ravages and pain of a disease like AIDS? Can *positive spiritual truths*, in essence, boost a person's beleaguered immune system—as Dr. Fountain claimed?

Immediately I thought of the many people I know with ailments related to a weakened, suppressed, or overwhelmed immune system—acquaintances who struggle daily with constant colds and allergies. Also rheumatoid arthritis, lupus, and other related disorders of the immune system. And what about those who suffer with chronic fatigue because their body is constantly at war with viruses, such as Epstein-Barr?

This inner climate—this positive approach to life—actually contributes to swifter healing from the emotional punches life throws.

As a healthcare professional, I had to know more about Dr. Fountain's findings. And I eagerly read on.

Fountain knew that recent studies have found a connection between what people believe and their physical health. If the human mind and body are so closely connected, he reasoned, why not try to help AIDS patients by having them focus their minds on God and his love? Why not help them to fill their thoughts with a belief in his power to heal?

Fountain began, he wrote, by incorporating the hospital's pastoral staff. They were encouraged to use wise counseling with AIDS patients when it came to emotional and spiritual issues—that is, they were to gently confront

fear, anger, doubt, and worry by helping patients refocus
their inner energies. They were to help people fix their
thoughts on the love of God demonstrated to us in Christ,
to believe in his healing power, and to build the conviction
that this power could touch and boost even a radically vi-
olated immune system. In short, the spirit was to be en-
listed in the effort to improve immune-system functioning. Dr. Fountain was not looking for miraculous cures
here, but he supposed that a positive, healthy spirit could
do nothing but foster a more healthy body. He wrote,

> Medical science is vigorously attacking the [HIV]
> virus, assuming that victory over the virus will solve
> the problem. . . . We . . . are working on the other side
> of the problem, with the immune system, trying
> through psycho-social-spiritual means to strengthen
> the immune system so it can better cope with the in-
> fection. Can it ever be sufficiently strengthened to
> eliminate the infection? As Paul wrote to the Colos-
> sians of Christ: "in whom are hidden all the treasures
> of wisdom and knowledge" (Colossians 2:3).[1]

I was really intrigued now. Was it possible to find people who had been helped toward better health—and even
healed of seemingly incurable illnesses—by learning to
build themselves up with a positive mind-set and with
spiritual truth? Could truth really recharge weakened immune systems? I wondered if Christian theologians had
yet done relevant work on this issue. What about scientists—did they have any hard data? Had any other doctors
tried programs similar to Dr. Fountain's, working with,
say, cancer, heart, or AIDS patients?

As I thought about it, it seemed to me that a very important fact is being largely ignored: *Some people recover
from the worst illnesses no matter how discouraging the sta-
tistics might be.* And an important two-part question is

rarely asked by the medical community: "Why do some who are supposed to die, live? And why do some who are supposed to live with chronic illnesses recover?"

Some time after reading Dr. Fountain's letter, I came across an arresting article run by the Associated Press. Dr. Stephen Ostroff, of The United States Center for Disease Control, declared that it is of supreme importance that we study both the physical *and* emotional condition of individuals who survive the deadly Ebola epidemic now raging in Africa. Said Dr. Ostroff, "Each individual who survives Ebola is very valuable." Now, it seemed, the official medical community was recognizing the crucial role that healthy spirituality plays in creating immune strength in people.

I was very excited to see that a healthcare professional with the standing of Dr. Ostroff was interested in learning how the mind and spirit can help people overcome chronic and fatal illnesses.

And so it was that I began to research the conditions that create inner health, and their connection with immune-boosting and physical health. That work has resulted in this book.

Today, I am convinced that strengthening your spirit with the bold, encouraging, life-giving truths that are revealed in the Bible—God's Word—will help you move toward physical wholeness and overall well-being.

But before you launch into the rest of the book, I'd like to share with you some wise cautions that I also encountered along the way.

Caution #1: "You're trying to analyze miracles and the miraculous," said a friend, "and I think that's a big mistake." He was partly right. You can't dissect miracles. He was also partly wrong. It's not miracles that I'll discuss in this book. I believe God heals miraculously today. And there is nothing to prevent his healing you miraculously if he wills to do so. But I want to present a clear picture of the process by which we separate illness-fostering untruths from the health-giving sense and wisdom of the truth. That truth grows out of the revelation of God in Jesus Christ.

What's the difference? you might ask.

A miracle, like the healing of the congenitally blind man (described in John 9), cannot be explained by the laws of nature as we know them: A miracle is entirely an act of God. Creating an inner climate that fosters health, on the other hand, involves our own efforts, things we can learn to do to help ourselves. I am referring to things like prayer, study, and meditation on the life-filled truths of the Bible. I believe we are *cooperating* with God when we create a healthy inner life—but it is, in essence, an entirely natural process. And as such, it may be scientifically demonstrated and analyzed. These effects result because God has designed our systems so that the thoughts and beliefs we activate in our minds *connect with our physical bodies.*

This notion is not new. Plato and Socrates, who lived nearly 500 years before Christ, had observed the mind-body connection and referred to its importance for sickness. Hippocrates, the father of medicine, said he would rather know what sort of person has a disease than what sort of disease the person has. Galen, a great Greek physician who lived in A.D. 140, wrote about the relationship he observed between depression and breast cancer. And Sir William Osler, a brilliant physician and medical history writer, said that the outcome of tuberculosis has more to do with what goes on in the patient than with what goes on in his lungs.

So I am not telling you that you can "create your own

miracle" or force God to create one for you. Anyone who says you can is in error.

Caution #2: I am not advocating "mind over matter" as do certain Christian cults; nor do I believe the New Age notion that you have mysterious latent powers that you can unleash. There is nothing here about ascended masters, pyramids, or crystals. Unfortunately, even some Christian writers have not bothered to distinguish these occult ideas from the facts of Scripture as they agree with recent scientific findings. In fact, I believe pursuing such things can seriously compromise your inner health because it introduces elements of false religion. The only safe guide to spiritual reality is God's revelation in Christ Jesus and in the sacred Scriptures. To be honest, that is one of the reasons I am writing this. I want to make a distinction between facts that have emerged from recent research and the abiding facts God has revealed to us about personal faith and healing.

Caution #3: It's a mistake to believe there is *no* connection between your beliefs and thoughts—which create inner moods and a life outlook—and the condition of your body's many intricate systems. Your immune system and several additional physical systems are in direct contact with your innermost thoughts. Therefore, to some extent, your body is subject to your influence and control. Now, thanks to recent research, we can trace some of the pathways between mind and body.

This means that you are not a mere victim of whatever pathological agents and processes happen to attack your body. Rather, you can employ your will to do something that will effectively move your body toward health. One of the most powerful agents of healing that you can control is your mind.

By learning to find and change pathological beliefs, thoughts, and attitudes, you can replace them with a truth-filled and healing mind-set. That means assuming some, but not all, of the *responsibility* for your health.

Caution #4: Don't give up on the program I will offer you in this book until you've tried it!

I have searched for, and found, the new evidence I set out to find about the mind-body connection. I am truly excited about what I've learned, and I want to share it with you.

If you work through this book doing the parts of the program that apply to you, you too can learn to help create an inner climate leading to physical health.

I've become convinced, as I hope you will, that true health must include spirit, mind, and body. I'm afraid too many of us in the healing professions have considered health to be a purely physical matter. But your efforts to heal, or to stay healthy, can be greatly improved by giving attention to the mind and spirit.

One final word: I am not saying that you should *substitute* attention to spirit, mind, and emotion for work with your physician, or for medication, exercise, and good nutrition. There are excellent books on nutrition and exercise. I recommend studying them because it's vital to include health-giving changes in these areas in any serious effort to improve your health or to get well.

Some of you have read other books of mine. Since I've been writing about *self-talk* and *truth* for about fifteen years, it's very likely that you have already learned something about the power of beliefs and thoughts as they affect our minds, emotions, and behavior. Now it's time to take a look at how changing your beliefs—about health and illness, death and dying, and attitudes of fear and resentment—can have powerful effects on your physical health. It's time to learn to change those thoughts that make you sick and to replace them with thoughts that can make you well.

If you're ready, let's work on it together now.

William Backus, Ph.D.
Licensed Psychologist
Forest Lake, Minnesota
January 1996

Notes

1. Personal communication, July 23, 1994.

Chapter 1

Rethinking Healthcare

Today's medical arsenal is stockpiled with wonder-drugs and powerful antibiotics. So imagine, if you can, an otherwise healthy eighteen-year-old spiraling toward death from tuberculosis—not the new, resistant strains we've heard about, but the old garden-variety disease, which is easily treatable. But then, something very strange was going on in John's life. He was a patient treated by Dr. Dan Fountain in Zaire.

John was admitted to a hospital with terrible pain in his right hip, a constant fever, and progressive weight loss. The doctors had no trouble with a diagnosis and began administering the proper antibiotic. But John's condition worsened, unexplainably. A month later, John appeared to be incurable. Doctors were mystified. He was dying.

One day, a student nurse took time from her busy schedule of studies and ward duties to have a leisurely talk with John. As she sat beside him, she was astounded to hear John say he was probably dying because he'd been *cursed.* An uncle, furious because a loan for the boy's schooling had not been repaid, told John, "You've been cursed. Very soon you'll become ill and die. Nothing that doctors can do will help you."

I am not suggesting that some supernatural power is released by such a curse. Rather, I see how a *persuaded mind* can influence the body. John believed in the curse, and his belief gave it power to take his life.

When the nurse told the story, the hospital team prayed for the wisdom to change John's *belief* in the curse. They led John to the Lord Jesus Christ, convinced him from the Scriptures that Jesus is mightier than his uncle's curse—and that Jesus did not want him to die. John accepted the truth about the reality of Christ's love for him, and his fear vanished. Now he was convinced that his uncle's curse could not harm him. The staff encouraged him to forgive his uncle. Forgiving brought inner release from anger, hatred, and bitterness.

John's body responded quickly to his new beliefs and the new, positive feelings. In just a few days John's fever left, and he began eating and gaining weight. Soon the tuberculosis that had been robbing him of life was gone.[1]

The Power of a Healthy Mind

Since learning of this case and others like it, I have come to realize what Jesus meant when he said, "The truth will make you free" (John 8:32). Along with freeing us from sin, I believe he meant to proclaim freedom from negative thoughts and their effects on our bodies. The physical improvement John experienced when he learned to tell himself the freeing truth has been given to many others too—including people with disorders like heart disease and cancer, and so-called incurable conditions like HIV infection. Strength and health can return for you too, even if you've been told there is no hope. If replacing negative thoughts with the truth does not bring you a rapid cure as it did in John's case, it can help you on the road to a healthier inner life, which will restore your life from within—no matter what your outer circumstances may be. On the other hand, you don't have to have a terrifying illness to make physical progress with the truth!

Pills, salves, injections, and surgery alone are not enough. You can learn a new way to cooperate with your own healing.

Perhaps you feel like a magnet for colds. Are you pestered every few weeks by a runny nose, a hacking cough, or plugged-up airways? Maybe you have a habit of coming down with everything that's "going around." Are you thinking of making "strep throat" your new middle name? Do you live with thyroid problems, blood sugar out of whack, stomach or intestinal disorders, ulcers? Are your emotions out of sync? Your symptoms or diagnosed diseases should not be neglected or handled without high-quality professional assistance. But as you may have discovered already, pills, salves, injections, and surgery alone are not enough. You can learn a new way to cooperate with your own healing. And that means discovering how to fill your mind with beliefs and thoughts that have tremendous therapeutic power.

Many people think they are slaves to their feelings. Others don't know it, but they are slaves just the same.

What you need is the courage and the will to change some habits—including perhaps your diet and exercise routine, rest and relaxation cycles, work and play habits. But the essence of the program I will outline throughout this book involves changing some of your *beliefs*, attitudes, and thought patterns and thus the inner climate they create. It is possible that some of your thoughts are making you susceptible to illness, or standing in the way of healing.

Thoughts and beliefs *can* make you sick. And thoughts can prevent optimal health. Especially thoughts that produce inner climates of *anger, fear, discouragement, bitterness, jealousy, frustration, discontent,* or *resentment.* That is because these negative patterns actually work to depress physiological processes, including the body's immune response. And that is a formula for disaster.

Thoughts Can Make People Sick

One goal of this program is to help you discover negative thought patterns that may be contributing to overall suppression of immune response, and to help you take a good look at behaviors and habits that may be working against you as well.

If you harbor the kinds of thoughts listed below, you are contributing to inner conditions that promote *poor* health—thoughts you can replace with ideas that affirm the goodness, love, and power of God:

- My case is hopeless.
- I might as well give up because the doctors can't help me.
- I can't help hating or resenting someone.
- I have nothing to look forward to but pain, suffering, and death.
- There is nothing I can do about the stress in my life.
- I cannot tolerate any type of frustration.
- My problems are overwhelming.
- Always expect the worst.

The following are some examples of behaviors and

habits that might be harming you. Some are practices or routines you need to change if you want to be healthy:

- avoiding other people, refusing to make friends, alienating yourself from others
- consuming a high-fat diet, eating too many saturated fats, not enough vegetables, fruits, whole grains, legumes
- neglecting to take necessary medications
- leading a sedentary lifestyle with too little exercise
- allowing too little time for breaks, rest, relaxation, and adequate sleep
- spending too little time in honest, open communication with God, whether in worship or private devotion
- practicing poor giving habits, serving others little or not at all
- smoking cigarettes, drinking too much, overeating, abusing drugs, indulging in illicit sexual activity.

Materialism: A Spiritual Disorder

If you are not convinced that your mind affects your body, you are not alone. Materialism, which infects our culture, is a narrow philosophy that still rules the thinking of many medical professionals. Doctors have been taught to think of themselves as sophisticated mechanics, repairing machines called "people." They aim weapons at germs, cancers, plaque, and chemical imbalances. For some disorders the materialistic approach works well. But the purely mechanical view has too many limits. Moreover, we know from God's revelation—and even from our own self-knowledge—that we are not machines.

Psychology, my own field, has also been infected with materialism. For years psychology has held that we cannot *know* anything about spiritual reality, absolute truth, or the meaning of life. When I was in graduate school, many psychologists believed optimistically that, because behavior was mechanically determined, we would soon be able to explain and control all human thoughts, feelings, and actions. All we needed was to learn more about how the "machine" worked. So it seemed puzzling that many of our patients wanted to talk about matters more profoundly significant to them than their weekly behavior-reinforcement schedules!

We are not machines. We must be treated as persons, not as mere collections of anatomical parts.

Such materialistic thinking represents a kind of "faith"—faith in mechanics, that is—which has been tried and found wanting. Much of this thinking still holds sway. Numerous psychologists, psychiatrists, and medical practitioners still cling to it. Maybe you have suspected that your own psychotherapist or physician thinks of you as a machine. If so, you may want to reconsider who you are working with in the care of your mind or body.

It is very important in personal health matters that we be treated as persons, and not as mere collections of anatomical parts.

"My doctor really did not want to hear about my feelings," one woman told her counselor. "As soon as I said I was depressed he cut me off, grabbed his prescription pad and wrote the name of an antidepressant. He told me to take one pill each night. Then he walked out on me. I felt like a machine."

This woman had sought psychological help because she didn't want to treat her problems as if they were nothing but chemical anomalies. No wonder so many of my patients say they don't want *pills* for their depression![2]

Following are some questions to consider to help you decide whether your physician has a broad enough view of your total health needs:

- Does your doctor take the time to talk with you and to listen to your concerns?
- Does she show interest in your marriage, your family, your work, and the impact of various life-factors on you?
- Does the doctor suggest that you use health aids like exercise, vacations, listening to music, talking to a counselor, or healthy socializing? Or does he prescribe a drug for every complaint?
- Is your therapist or physician interested in your spiritual life, giving due recognition to the fact that church attendance, prayer, and other spiritual practices have been shown to be important risk factors? If you are not satisfied that this person is willing to take spiritual realities seriously and to respect your beliefs and your feelings, you may want to find someone who does.

Are You Working With Your Doctor, or Taking Orders?

It's important for you to know that you are working *with*, not *against*, your doctor or therapist. You are not required to work *under* the doctor's authority, like a soldier under a commanding officer. For best results, your psychological and medical treatment must be considered your responsibility, not someone else's. If you have a condition requiring treatment, you need competent professional help. But you need to view your professional person as one who informs, advises, and assists you in making decisions that will promote your health aims and recovery.

Powerful help is often available through appropriate use of many kinds of skilled professionals, such as chiropractic doctors, surgeons, psychiatrists, psychologists, or the use of allopathic medicine. I am suggesting that you also consider the crucial spiritual, mental, emotional, and behavioral contributions that go into creating health.

———————

Now we need to return to some questions raised by the story of eighteen-year-old John, whose belief in a curse made him ill. How did belief in Jesus make him well again? How did his encounter with truths contained in the Bible impact the fears that were killing him? Has research demonstrated that connections between mind and body exist—that thoughts, feelings, and beliefs really affect our physical organs and make us sick or healthy?

The medical community is on the threshold of breakthrough thinking and discoveries. Let's take a look now at this new frontier.

Notes

1. From a personal communication by Dr. Dan Fountain, M.D.
2. Antidepressants are effective against depression insofar as it has a biochemical component. But *physical* treatments are often not enough. Depression is a case in point. While it responds to pills in many cases, it can recur more readily if it's treated with *nothing but* pills. Treatment with changed beliefs and thoughts can bring not only recovery but resistance to recurrence.

Chapter 2

Your Spirit, and You

Pop-scientist Carl Sagan wrote: "My fundamental premise about the brain is that its workings ... are a consequence of its anatomy and physiology, and nothing more."

And nothing more? What about man's soul?

Sagan and others in the scientific community are wrong when they make grand pronouncements of this nature. Expertise in the physical sciences does not qualify you to speak with special authority in other fields. For decades we've allowed science and the medical community to make ultimate pronouncements. But science cannot discover ultimates. If humans are to have knowledge about our complex physical/spiritual nature, it has to come from what the Creator has revealed. Philosophers can speculate, but only God can articulate the ultimate truth about what we are—matter *and* spirit, physical *and* non-material. We are wrong if we allow the purely materialistic to tell us about ultimate answers and realities. Only One can tell us about ultimates, and that is God.

Because the non-material aspects of creation cannot be known through our senses, we must learn about them from the Scriptures. There we discover the truth about ourselves: we are creatures with a material body and a non-material soul and spirit.[1] This merging of matter and spirit creates the mind-body challenge, raising the question: How are spirit, mind, and body related to one another?

Philosophers can speculate, but only God can articulate the ultimate truth about what we are—matter *and* spirit, physical *and* non-material. Only One can tell us about ultimate answers and realities, and that is God.

The Human Spirit

You have a spirit, and it is joined to the rest of you in such a way that your spirit communicates with your mind, and your mind communicates with your body. The spirit is a receptacle originally designed by the Creator as an abiding place for his Holy Spirit. It is that part of a person that seeks restlessly until it finds its rest in God. Your spirit is that part of you that communicates its empty restlessness to your mind, until you find yourself asking those ultimate questions: "Where am I going?" "Who am I?" "Where have I come from?" "Why am I here?" The questions prompted by man's spirit are those to which only God can give true answers. But since the fall everyone who is born of the flesh is born with an empty spirit. Only through a new birth by faith in Jesus Christ can we be filled again with God's Spirit, so that our inner man comes alive to a new world and new possibilities, from a world of the Spirit beyond our natural senses. How are we to think of these new possibilities, which we perceive with our spirit, while physical sense and science tell us to pay attention only to the physical, material world?

Enter—the *mind*. The mind is thought, will, and emotion. I like the figure invented by the great brain surgeon Dr. Wilder Penfield, who argued that the brain is a computer programmed by the mind.[2] You can think of your brain as an instrument, like a piano. Your non-material spirit and mind play it in order to express themselves in the physical world. *Not only do the spirit and mind influence the body's actions, they profoundly affect your body's health.*

Recently scientists have demonstrated conclusively that the mind has a powerful effect on the health or illness of the body. This influence is great enough to help make you sick or help you get well. Changes in your spirit affect your mind and changes in your mind can affect your body.

Most often illness results from several interacting causes. For instance, what do you think is the cause of peptic ulcers? You may be thinking: "Overwork." Or if you are in touch with the latest thought on the subject, you might have said, "A bacteria." These are the two popular *theories* about the cause of ulcers, and of general stomach irritations as well. But the truth is that some people have lots of the bacteria in question growing in their digestive tract but have no peptic disturbance whatsoever. And the world is full of ulcer-free men and women who thrive on hard work. The evidence suggests that it is people who create inward spiritual turmoil for themselves—producing perpetual anxiety, irritability, or resentment—*and* who have the *H. pylori* bacteria growing in their intestines who are more likely to have stomach troubles and ulcers. Stress normally can't do the nasty job by itself, nor can the bacteria acting alone. Why do we insist on thinking of disease as having just one cause? Why do we continue emphasizing everything but the mind when we consider causes? Why don't we learn to think of several interacting causes instead of narrowly considering a single material agent? Probably because of the influence of materialists, who often try to reduce every illness to one lone cause, and try to come up with one magic-bullet cure.

Not long ago a psychological journal ran a list of medical problems associated with anxiety. The length of the list bowled me over, including such medical disorders as arrhythmia, hypertension, asthma, hyperventilation syndrome, migraines, muscle spasms, temperomandibular joint syndrome (TMJ), irritable bowel syndrome (IBS), motility disorders . . . and many more. Anxiety is something we create with our minds when we tell ourselves an event or condition is a terrible threat to us and that the dreaded thing is highly likely to occur. Nobody is saying anxiety is the sole cause of the disorders on the list but that it can conspire with other causes to create disease.

Why do we insist on thinking of disease as having just one cause? Why do we continue emphasizing everything but the mind when we consider causes? Why don't we learn to think of several interacting causes instead of narrowly considering a single material agent?

A number of years ago, before changes in health insurance plans made it difficult for our clinic to offer biofeedback training at a reasonable cost, we used a simple technique to treat anxiety-related cold hands. We taught people how to use their minds to dilate the tiny blood vessels in their hands, which warmed them. It was a simple matter of teaching them to relax and control the tension that had choked the blood supply to their fingers. Most people can learn to use their minds to warm their fingers and toes. It's not mystical and it's not spooky. It is a rudimentary demonstration that God has built connections between the mind and body, connections that can also be effective in boosting immune response and creating overall good health. Many studies have now documented the positive potential of the mind to influence the body.

For instance, a 1995 report summarized a study of 93 men infected with HIV. The study revealed that severe life stress made the patients get worse while those who eluded similar stresses remained more healthy in spite of their infection.[3]

More scientists are looking closely at what the mind can do. Dr. George Engel at the University of Rochester Medical Center recounts examples of what he has called the "giving-up complex." He has observed how a defeated spirit and a hopeless mental attitude combine to cause a person's body to shut down immune responses. Among other examples, Dr. Engel tells of a woman who lived with a severely abusive husband. She was convinced she could not leave him but she was just as certain she could not continue to live with him. She told herself that there was no escape, that her situation was hopeless. Despite the fact that she had no fatal physical disease, the woman developed a breathing difficulty, and although she received the very best physical treatment in a fine hospital, she died.[4]

Jean Charcot, a nineteenth-century French neurologist who understood the life-enhancing power of the non-material mind, said, "The best inspirer of hope is the best physician."[5]

What Hopelessness Can Do

Dr. Blair Justice, a writer who has carefully explored the mind-body connection, believes there is evidence to prove the power of hope and hopelessness. It appears that people who define their situation as hopeless may cause their own bodies to conserve too much oxygen—like people trying to hold their breath. The vagal-nerve reaction this triggers can slow the heart until it stops and the patient dies—literally dies of hopelessness![6]

Numerous experiments have been conducted comparing large groups of people who often get sick with similar groups who do not. For instance, one group of over a thousand telephone operators was divided into those who became ill very often and those who were seldom sick. Those who were sick frequently were chronically more disgruntled and unfulfilled than those who seldom got sick. Furthermore, the discontented group experienced their illnesses in batches—clustered together at times when they were having an especially tough time coping with problems in living. The experimenters have this to say about germs, toxins, and other environmental "causes" to which we have customarily attributed most illnesses:

> So far as we have been able to determine, physical hardship, geographic and climatic change, and changing exposure to toxic or infectious agents, *are not the significant variables*. Only occasionally does it appear that the development of an isolated illness, or a cluster of illnesses, is simply the result of some fortuitous encounter with bacteria, trauma, or other influences arising from the physical environment(emphasis mine).[7]

The widely cited experience of Dr. Bruno Klopfer also illustrates this point. Klopfer treated a patient, whose cancer had metastasized, with a drug called Krebiozen, thought to be a cancer cure. Since that time Krebiozen has been demonstrated to be ineffective—but both Klopfer and his patient *thought* they were using a new wonder-drug and were excited and hopeful. As soon as Klopfer administered Krebiozen the patient's tumors "melted like snowballs." Free of disease, the patient went his way. But a few months later newspaper headlines announced that Krebiozen had absolutely no effect on cancer. Upon reading the story, this patient's growths came back.

Now Klopfer decided to try a new tack. Having witnessed the power of the patient's beliefs, he informed the man that he was giving him a more potent form of Krebiozen, one that was known to be very effective. Instead he injected his patient with distilled water. But the patient *believed* he had been given the proverbial "magic bullet." The cancer vanished.

A few months later this man read of new, conclusive research that proved Krebiozen was worthless. He fell into hopeless despair. At once the cancer returned, and he died.

God's Word vs. New Age Mentality

What are we who are Christians to make of this? In a word, we are wise to resist "mind sciences" and occult thinking.

But there is nothing "New Age" in understanding that a world of non-material reality exists, and that hopelessness is a spiritual malady that afflicts the mind, causing despairing thoughts—and ultimately impacting the material body. It is rather a basic tenet of the teachings of Jesus. He cautioned us not to fear people who have power to destroy our body, because the spirit is beyond their reach. Conversely, he repeatedly told people whose bodies were restored to health, "Your *faith* has made you well!" Of course, their faith was placed in Christ and in his power to heal.

Why should we be shocked that scientists are noting that our state of mind has power to touch and influence the body?

But let's make some clear distinctions. The New Age mentality says, "Since your mind can affect your material body, it can affect everything. For this reason 'you are god—you can do anything!' " Jesus gave us no license to imagine ourselves in the role of a deity. We are to be firmly, completely submitted to the direction and rule of God himself, not to "mind power." As he said, "Rather, fear him who has power to destroy both body and soul in hell."

Remember, you and I are *not* God. We cannot do everything!

Nonetheless, we can cooperate with him in maintaining good health, or in healing. This may require a careful examination of the contents of your innermost heart—that place where your real attitudes toward life are to be found (see Proverbs 4:23).

Yes, we are more than physical bodies; we are spirit. But recognizing that we are spiritual beings in a physical body is not enough. What is *in* our spirit matters a great deal.

For the next several chapters we will look at important changes in the scientific community's views—especially where it comes to the connection between a healthy inner state and the physical body. I believe it is important for you to understand that revolutionary changes in thinking are taking place.

Then we'll be ready to develop a personalized program for you—one that can create a healthy inner climate, *and* boost your immune resistance, *and* add up to a healthier you!

Notes

1. You can find the terms *spirit* and *soul* used throughout the Bible, where their meanings appear to be anything but precise. However loosely these words may have been applied by various people at various times, they very clearly do not refer to the body. There are, for example, many places where the reference is to a *non-material component* in the human being: *spirit* in Psalm 31:5, Luke 23:46, Luke 24:37–39; *soul* in Matthew 10:28, 16:26; *spirit, soul,* and *body* in 1 Thessalonians 5:23.

2. Wilder Penfield, O.M., LITT.B., M.D., F.R.S., *The Mystery of the Mind: A Critical Study of Consciousness and the Human Brain* (Princeton, N.J.: University Press, 1979), pp. 57–59.

3. From a study reported to the May 1995 meeting of the American Psychiatric Association by Dr. John Petitto of the University of South Florida, Gainesville.

4. Herbert Benson, M.D., *The Mind-Body Effect* (New York: Simon & Schuster, 1979). This case was reported to Dr. Engel by Dr. Leon J. Saul of Media, Pennsylvania.

5. Ibid.

6. Blair Justice, Ph.D., *Who Gets Sick: How Beliefs, Moods, and Thoughts Affect Your Health* (Los Angeles: Jeremy P. Tarcher, Inc. and Houston: Peak Press). Distributed by St. Martin's Press, New York, 1988.

7. L. E. Hinkle and H. G. Wolff, Ecologic investigations of the relationship between illness, life experiences, and the social environment, *Annals of Internal Medicine* (1958): 49, 1373–1388. Cited in Blair Justice, *Who Gets Sick: How Beliefs, Moods, and Thoughts Affect Your Health.*

Chapter 3

Hurtful Words, Helpful Words

For many years medical and psychological researchers largely avoided studying the impact of religious faith and spiritual well-being on physical health. Textbooks never even referred to the few studies that were available. Today, revolutionary thinking in this area is just beginning to affect us—because doctors have discovered that the spiritual life *does* have a proven influence on health and healing.

Recently many studies have revealed the positive impact of spiritual reality on physical illnesses. Researchers have found, for instance, that cardiovascular disease, gastrointestinal disorders, many forms of cancer, and hypertension are not as common among religious people as they are among people with little or no faith.[1] True, some of the positive results in these studies are traceable to the disciplined lifestyles of believers. Yet the beliefs of the faithful are the source of self-discipline and healthful habits. And constructive inner-life habits, such as forgiveness and generosity, are proving to have healthful benefits as well.

John's story, as recorded in Chapter 1, is not an isolated incident. Other superstition-generated illnesses and healings have been well-documented. Effective as "spells" and "curses" are in causing illness and even death, their power is not supernatural. It is the victim's culturally transmitted "faith" in the power of the curse that does him in. John was indeed blessed that his doctors, nurses, and pastoral counselors knew the truth that trusting in Jesus Christ overcomes every power—real or imagined.

Now, you might argue against using John's story because it happened in Africa. We think that here in our Western culture a curse would have little effect because we are "free" of mind influences, such as superstitions. And in a sense Christianity and its liberating truths *have* had the effect of freeing us from such influences—though much of the popular culture now rejects Christianity's truths. But what cannot be accomplished in the West by a relative's muttered curse might be achieved by words from other sources of "power," such as a medical professional's prognostic death sentence.

"Stay Away From Us!"

Paul Pearsall, like many of the people I want to tell you about, recovered from cancer. He wrote about the Western version of the uncle's curse—a doctor's pronouncement of doom:

> When I was struggling with cancer a few years ago . . . a doctor one day brought particularly frightening news. Gazing at his clipboard, he murmured, "It doesn't look like you're going to make it."
> Before I could ask a question, my wife stood up, handed me my robe, and adjusted the tubes attached to my body. "Let's get out of here. This man is a risk to your health," she said. As she helped me struggle

to the door the doctor approached us. "Stay back," demanded my wife. "Stay away from us."

As we walked together down the hall the doctor attempted to catch up with us. "Keep going," said my wife, pushing the intravenous stand. "We're going to talk to someone who really knows what's going on." Then she held up her hand to the doctor. "Don't come any closer to us. . . ."

We fled to safety—and to hope—with a doctor who did not confuse diagnosis with verdict. I could never have made that walk toward wellness alone.[2]

Paul Pearsall lived to benefit from his wife's wisdom. If you are convinced that your disease is bound to kill you, the fact is your belief might speed up the process. In fact, it might be possible to die from telling yourself you have no hope rather than from the disease itself. If you find yourself in the care of a healer who has no interest in helping you toward hopefulness, truth, and emotional victory, get away fast.

Religious Purveyors of Doom

Even those who undertake spiritual ministries for the healing of sick persons can function instead as religious purveyors of doom. This negative focus created the plight of a woman I'll call Shirley who wrote to me on the Internet. Crippled with rheumatoid arthritis, Shirley was told by people in her church that the illness was her own fault—the result of sins she had failed to confess, of allowing demons to oppress her, and of failing to spend enough time reading the Bible. At first she took these admonitions seriously. Far from enjoying improvement, though, Shirley found herself becoming nearly immobilized by her worsening joint pains and swelling. At last she left that church and joined another one, where she found emotional and spiritual support. Hope returned. Sure enough, she began to improve. "I believe the ministry I found in my new church is the foundation of my physical healing," she says.

I believe her.

It is very hard for your body to flourish when hope is dashed by someone whom you trust—such as fellow believers or medical experts.

After a day of tests at a teaching hospital, Reid Henson and his wife entered the room where the doctor was shuffling through his files. They were virtually ignored while the man thumbed through his papers. "All of a sudden," Henson says, "the doctor jumped out of his seat, ran into the hallway, and shouted to another doctor, 'Hey, Rick, we've got another hairy cell leukemia here. And I diagnosed it over the phone. What do you think about that?' That's how I found out I had cancer."[3] Needless to say, Henson's progress toward health began *later*, when he found someone who did not confuse a human being suffering from an illness with a diagnostic category—someone who understood that belief and hope make a crucial difference.

Upbeat Beliefs and Strong Support

As I said at the outset of this book, the content of your spirit *does* matter when it comes to your physical health.

When we begin to receive new beliefs and positive support, we improve the conditions that foster health. Both positive beliefs and supportive brothers and sisters can be found in some churches. So we should expect people who go to church and who believe and practice the good news heard there to have better health than those who do not. As noted earlier, careful research demonstrates that people who attend church regularly have less cardiovascular disease, less pulmonary emphysema, less cirrhosis of the liver, less abnormal cervical cell formation, and lower blood pressure than people who do not go to church often. Similar benefits have been shown to result from prayer and increased faith. That is because attention to spiritual truth changes our thinking, and we realize we have hope and divine love and assistance from outside the realm of fallen nature.

In other words, the health benefits of Christian faith and practice are tangible and measurable. New life and new realities are open to us.

When you and I come into fellowship with the Holy Trinity through the new birth and faith in Jesus Christ, we receive many powerful new "facts of life." One of the great new facts is that we are no longer alone. Rather, we have fellowship with the Father and with Jesus himself as well as with our spiritual brothers and sisters. This can make a difference in our health, because when social contact is increased and loneliness is reduced the immune system seems to grow stronger and health and longevity get a boost. Apparently it is important to know we are not isolated and "all by ourselves." Even more vital, the support of other people helps us to hang on to the positives and believe the truth. When social contact is increased the immune system appears to strengthen. Even having a dog or cat for company seems to improve health in some individuals. That is because companionship—even that of an animal—can help us believe we are not abandoned to ourselves.

Knowing that others care for and support us is essential to health.

A study of stress at the University of Chicago highlighted the fact that among business executives exposed to stressful situations, those who stayed healthy—those the experimenters called "hardy executives"—were people who *believed* they were in control and that the stressful event was a positive challenge. And what helped them to believe this and react in this way were friends or relatives who supported them, and the effect was major.

Executives who did not have positive beliefs and supportive fellowship had more than nine chances in ten of becoming severely ill in the near future while the first group had *less than one chance in ten* of developing severe sickness any time soon.[4] The major impact determining illness or health for these people was in their minds. *What they told themselves about their circumstances made the difference.*

Yes, the content of your spirit really can change things. A limited, self-centered, and materialistic view of life does not embrace the truth. There is a wealth of help and possibility outside our own small world—the realm inhabited by a God of truth who cares about us and our circumstances.

If we have a God who cares about us, it would be wise to take a look at what he says about the connection between a healthy spirit and a healthy body—and about the human spirit in general.

Notes

1. Peter C. Hill and Eric M. Butler, "The role of religion in promoting physical health," *Journal of Psychology and Christianity*, 14, 2, 141–155.
2. Paul Pearsall, "Laws of Lasting Love," *Reader's Digest*, (March 1995): 147ff.
3. See Reid Henson's story as told by himself in O. Carl Simonton, M.D. and Reid M. Henson, with Brenda Hampton, *The Healing Journey* (New York: Bantam Books, 1992.)

4. S. R. Maddi and S. C. Kobasa, *The Hardy Executive: Health Under Stress* (Homewood, Ill.: Dow, Johannes-Irwin, 1984.) Cited in Blair Justice, Ph.D., *Who Gets Sick: How Beliefs, Moods, and Thoughts Affect Your Health* (Los Angeles: Jeremy P. Tarcher, Inc. and Houston: Peak Press), Distributed by St. Martin's Press, New York, 1988.

Chapter 4

State of the Heart

The first person ever to recover from AIDS is, reportedly, William Calderone. Diagnosed with AIDS in 1982, Calderone was given a death sentence. Doctors told him he would probably be dead in six months. He became hopeless, depressed, and sick. His body was soon covered with the cancerous skin eruptions of Kaposi's sarcoma.

Then an extraordinary thing happened. A friend looked him in the eye and said, "You don't have to die." Calderone began a program that included changing his beliefs and mental imagery, confronting negative self-talk, maintaining a healthy diet, and exercise. Calderone's health improved, the tumors shrank, and two years later he showed *no signs of AIDS*.[1]

A January 24, 1995, story by Lawrence K. Altman in the New York *Times*[2] reveals that Calderone's case, though rare, is not unique, in that some others—no one knows for certain how many—though infected with HIV, do not become ill. Even though the lethal virus has inhabited their bodies for years, they develop no disease signs. These people are aglow with health. Newton L. Butler, for instance, has been infected with the virus for ten or fifteen years, yet he has developed no symptoms and none of the opportunistic infections that ordinarily weaken and finally kill victims of the disease. Butler's immune system's functioning has been well within normal range. Such long-term survivors are called "non-progressors," and the reasons for their well-being are presently unknown to investigators.

If you ask Butler what has helped him, he will tell you that he determined to take charge of his own health and not to wait passively for doctors and the government to make him well. Butler set up his own self-management regimen. In addition to developing a take-charge attitude, Butler never smokes, he exercises regularly, he limits his alcohol intake to a glass of wine once in a while, and he takes as few medications as possible.

Why are some people sick and others well? Why is it that even the most virulent plagues don't kill everyone who gets sick with them? At this writing, an outbreak of Ebola virus in Africa has dominated the news headlines, so deadly is this pathogen. Yet, according to spokespersons for the World Health Organization, while ninety percent of Ebola virus victims die a horrible death, we can't avoid noticing that one in ten survives. Why is this?

The old materialistic bio-medical theory, still held by some, argues that each disease has one pathogen (causal factor). One disease, one cause. Is it true? Is the difference between the sick and the well due to the presence or absence of a virus or bacteria? Not entirely. Some people, like William Calderone and Newton Butler, harbor pathogenic microorganisms in their bodies and do not get sick. Some eat fat and cholesterol all their lives and stay well.

Some people generate cancerous cells but do not develop cancer.

Recently, Minnesota health officials announced that four people died from streptococcus bacteria, an organism transported by tens of thousands of children. Most of these do not even develop invasive strep—and most of those who do, do not die. Each year 10,000 to 15,000 people develop the illness—and 2,000 of them die. What is the difference between those who die and those who survive? Why some and not others? Is it simply a mystery like predestination? Some authorities are even questioning whether HIV can be the sole cause of AIDS.[3] This is a crucial question in view of the fact that some people have been infected with HIV for five, ten, even twenty years *without developing symptoms of AIDS*. In fact, according to some estimates, for every living adult with AIDS there are 100 to 300 people infected with HIV *with no disease*. Among those who suffer from virtually any terminal illness, some do not die as they are "supposed" to.

The old materialistic bio-medical theory, still held by some, argues that each disease has one pathogen (causal factor). One disease, one cause. Is it true?

An Ancient and Potent Prescription

You might be surprised to learn that the Bible may have some answers. The Bible speaks of the power of a healthy inner spirit, as Solomon noted:

A merry heart doeth good like a medicine: but a broken spirit drieth the bones. Proverbs 17:22, KJV

Examine this selection of Bible passages and see how

What Is Your "Inner Climate"?

Most of us carry a kind of base-line attitude toward life in general. Surely you've been in a room when someone walks in and things "brighten up," or "the room goes cold," as we say. We all know people who, on the whole, have been gloomy all their lives, or indomitable in spirit no matter what odds were stacked against them.

How about you? What is the "inner climate" of your soul like, on the whole? To help you get a general idea, here's one way to think about your inner weather patterns:

Frigid:

Generally depressive, or chronically depressed. Hopeless about the future and life itself. Full of constant regrets, or feeling that the best of life is already over—or that life "passed you by." You carry a lot of offenses that, for other people, would have been forgotten a long time ago.

Torrid:

You feel "hot" at someone most of the time. Irritation, annoyance persist like the "dog days" of summer. If you're honest with yourself, those occasional flare-ups of anger are scary or embarrassing. You think about getting back a lot—because you feel "burned" you want to scorch the other guy.

What Is Your Inner Climate? (continued)

Temperate:

Some weather patterns roll in from the Frigid Zone, and move out quickly. That's because you take the time to figure out the problem and deal with it as best you can—not just shrug it off. Likewise, those blasts from the Torrid Zone—because you deal with the sources of your anger. Quite literally, you "work them out," that is, out of *you*. As a result, you have many times when life feels mostly good and new, or golden and abundant with achievements, personal happinesses, and intact friendships.

Desert:

Mostly, you feel bored with life, dry in spirit. No taste for friends, fun, or intellectual stimulus. You carry an inner sense that most of the so-called joys of life turn out to be "mirages"—empty illusions not worth pursuing. But you deeply long for inner fulfillment . . . if only you knew what it tasted like, and where to find it.

Recognize any of these? Most of us can identify with the whole range of these emotional states—but you may find that one characterized you most of the time.

You can do something about your inner climate. Think about it.

God's Word assumes there is a spirit-mind-body connection, and observe its results:

- When I kept silent, my bones wasted away through my groaning all day long. For day and night your hand was heavy upon me; my strength was sapped as in the heat of summer (Psalm 32:3–4).
- For my days vanish like smoke; my bones burn like glowing embers. My heart is blighted and withered like grass; I forget to eat my food. Because of my loud groaning I am reduced to skin and bones (Psalm 102:3–5).
- A man's spirit sustains him in sickness, but a crushed spirit who can bear? (Proverbs 18:14).

Here health and illness are ascribed to the state of the human heart—to our inner state. These and other passages reveal and confirm a profound truth—that a positive, bright spirit is like a deflective shield, boosting our physical well-being. People who learn how to make this truth work for them have ways of coping with strong negative emotions, which otherwise have power to make them sick.

The power seems to begin working for us when we decide to do whatever it takes to change a negative inner climate. For instance, when Jesus intended to heal a man who was paralyzed, he began by setting the man's conscience free: "Take heart, son," he said first, "your sins are forgiven."[4] Remarkable words! Coming from him, they would make a guilt-ridden heart lighter indeed. Now, it's true that Jesus was about to perform a physical miracle, but he also knew it was important to offer a spiritual prescription to cure *guilt, fear, hopelessness,* even *self-hatred.* Jesus understood that diagnosing a person's inner state and consequent emotions is as important as changing the physical factors contributing to an illness. Yes, physical factors affect our health, and medications are useful. But doctors have long behaved as though spiritual ailments were unimportant—things such as hidden sin, guilt, shame, regret, fear, anger, resentment, bitterness, and cynicism. But they can and do play a causal role in sickness. In the vivid language of the Psalms, poor spiritual health dries up the bones like a summer drought.

If the joy of the Lord can supply people with the strength to rebuild a city wall,[5] then positive *self-talk* and its accompanying spiritual lift can contribute to radiant physical well-being.

Jesus understood that diagnosing a person's inner state and consequent emotions is as important as changing the physical factors contributing to an illness.

God Heals Believers—a Routine Benefit of Faith

Like many believers, I once thought that whenever the Bible spoke of God's healing power, it always only referred to miracles—those sudden and wondrous changes from sickness to health that sometimes occur in response to prayer. Miracles are exceptional events, and we cannot explain them except as "acts of God."

Some well-meaning Christians see God's promise to preserve the health of his people, as recorded in Exodus and Deuteronomy, as a pledge to perform miracles routinely. Moreover, they think that by "claiming" these promises they can unleash miracle-power as if by magic from heaven. I do not believe this is biblical.

Rather, I believe that the Exodus and Deuteronomy promises *assume* that God's people will live in a relaxed

state of trust—a state of inner peace and rest and obedience. Because of this inner condition of complete trust
they will listen carefully to God's Word of truth and accept
what he calls good and reject what he calls bad. Ultimately
this will lead to better health for his people, a state of health
superior to that of other nations. For example, Exodus
15:26 seems to explain that there is something naturally
healthful about hearing and doing God's commands: "If
you diligently heed the voice of the LORD your God and
do what is right in His sight, give ear to His commandments and keep all His statutes, I will put none of the diseases on you which I have brought on the Egyptians. For
I am the LORD who heals you" (NKJV).[6]

Do these passages promise you a *miracle* whenever you
are sick? I don't think so. Miracles and instant healings
through prayer do happen today, but these passages and
others like them offer another route to physical blessing.
They promise that the truth of God as it is conveyed in
Scripture has power to help you move toward healing if
you are sick, or to help you stay well if you are presently
in good health. The truth will work effectively only insofar
as you tell it to yourself—and only so far as you carry it
out in your actions. To put it another way, *The truth has a
positive impact on our bodies when it is believed and when it
is allowed to change our state of heart—that is, our moods and
character.*

The Role of the Mind

Over the past ten to fifteen years, researchers have
been learning much about the amazing effect of the mind
on the body. And that has led many to observe the amazing effect of the internal monologue—or *self-talk*—and the
resulting feelings, moods, and actions as it relates to the
body. Two truths that have emerged from scientific study

of these issues by investigators[7] are these:

(1) Most diseases do not result from a single causal factor.

(2) Even so-called "terminal" illnesses are not, in themselves, sufficient to cause death.

Nutrition, exercise, and rest make a significant difference, as does a sense of belonging to a group of other people. But most significant for our purposes is the exciting recognition by scientific medicine that people's attitudes, beliefs, and self-talk can make them sick or well, preserve life or cause death. These findings concur with the ancient teachings of the Bible.

Two truths that have emerged from scientific study of these issues by investigators are these:

Most diseases do not result from a single causal factor.

Even so-called "terminal" illnesses are not, in themselves, sufficient to cause death.

As we've noted, there are other factors in maintaining or gaining health. But the mind has an important influence on improved physical health—an influence that has often been neglected.

How does this influence really work?

We can gain insight into the mind-body connection by taking a careful look at one of the body systems most affected by positive and negative inner states: the immune system.

Perhaps you've never had a glimpse inside one of the

most fascinating systems God ever created. You will be delightfully surprised. . . .

Notes

1. Bernie S. Siegel, M.D., *Love, Medicine, and Miracles* (New York: Harper & Row, 1990), p. 39. Dr. Siegel cites as his source a discussion of Calderone's case by Jean Shinoda Bolen, M.D., in *New Realities* (March–April 1985): pp. 9–15. Siegel's work on the powerful contribution of mind, emotion, and attitude to healing, while very creative and often helpful is unfortunately impaired by the inclusion of pantheistic New Age religious speculation.
2. Lawrence K. Altman, "Long-Term Survivors May Hold Key Clues to Puzzle of AIDS." This story was taken from the Internet.
3. Several highly respected scientists have challenged the theory that HIV is the cause of AIDS. Two of the leading critics have published a book setting out their arguments. I do not know the answer to this question, but for readers who want to look into the issue, here is the reference: Bryan Ellison and Peter Duesberg, *Why We Will NEVER Win the War on AIDS* (Visalia, Calif.: Inside Story Communications), Dept. A, 1525 E. Noble, #102, Visalia, CA 93292.
4. Matthew 9:2
5. Nehemiah 8:10
6. See also Deuteronomy 7:12–15. These passages are capable of adding a powerful new dimension to the old "one physical cause" theory of medicine. Incidentally, good physicians have never really thought a person's thoughts, feelings, and behaviors were immaterial. Galen, Hippocrates, and many other great physicians of the past have known what we are saying here.
7. Experimental scientists such as Joan Borysenko, Suzanne

Kobasa, and J. K. Kiecolt-Glaser, as well as writers such as Herbert Benson, Barbara Brown, and Blair Justice, are among many who have conducted research on the mind-body connection.

Chapter 5

Your Own Private Arsenal

Most of us go through life without giving a thought to the secret weapon God planted inside us. Built into every one of us is equipment that is designed to give us incredible protection from disease.

Would this equipment—your immune system—work better if you deliberately gave it more attention? Some people have tried, with impressive results.

You and I *can* help ourselves by making better use of our pre-installed equipment! I want to help you understand how our body's protective system works and how it teams up with the mind. Then we can look at our feelings and self-talk—and some good living habits—that we can use for our own well-being.

Your Own Bodyguards

Many house-hunting germs consider your body exactly the home they're looking for. It's warm, cozy, and comfortable, and stocked with ample supplies of food and drink. Although your body doesn't like these foreign invaders, they continually try to break in. But don't be alarmed. You have excellent "bodyguards" living inside you. Their job is to keep out invaders, or get rid of them when they manage to squeeze inside. These guys are the cells of your immune system, a virtual army that can fend off invasions by alien microorganisms (viruses, bacteria, fungi, parasites, or protozoa), toxic materials (a foreign protein, carbohydrate, or nucleic acid)—or even a cell of your own that has become malignant.

These cell-characters, like human bodyguards, are primed to attack unwanted substances and get rid of them. Even if you don't know much about germs and diseases, your immune system does. It can recognize millions of different kinds of invaders and use the right weapons to rid your body of their unwelcome advances.

You have excellent "bodyguards" living inside you. Their job is to keep out invaders, or get rid of them when they manage to squeeze inside.

This is what happens when the immune system in your body spots an invader, a cell, or a germ that doesn't belong there: The "guard" cells, lots of them, pass the word to each other that a foreign substance is present. An alarm goes out and other powerful cells are directed to attack and destroy the invader. These cells communicate with each other so the word spreads rapidly.

B Cells, T Cells, and Phagocytes

As we noted, the name for immune system cells is lymphocytes, some of which are called B cells. These guys make antibodies, which attack viruses, bacteria, and cells distorted by cancer and mark them for destruction. Other special cells in your immune system are called T cells—and one kind of T cell is called a *killer T cell*. Killers get rid of cells that have been infected by germs or become cancerous. Their mission is to secrete powerful chemicals that are lethal to trouble-making prowlers.

Some of the cells in your immune system do away with invaders by eating them. They are called *phagocytes* (Greek for *cell-eaters*). Some are really big eaters. Phagocytes travel around and consume debris, worn-out cells, and other unwelcome components.

How It All Works

Now for a look at the system in action.

Let's imagine that trouble is brewing. What do you suppose is most often the cause when our bodies get sick? The answer is *infection*. The result can be as simple as the sniffles and sneezes we call a *cold*, or something much worse, such as *hepatitis*. Suppose some tiny microbes try to get in and cause an infectious disease. This is what will happen:

First, the invader has to get past your outer coat of armor—your skin. It isn't easy. Skin and the membranes lining the openings to your body are full of immune defenses, like antibodies and other defending cells. If the interloper makes it past the skin, it will face an army of *natural killer cells* (NK cells) which pose a formidable threat. After that, your body will call up its other bodyguards—antibodies and other cells, which are able to identify exactly what the invader is like and do away with it. If your body has had to deal with this particular kind of invader in the past, either through once having had the disease, or by vaccination, some of your T cells and B cells will "re-

Need a Boost?

Certain vitamins are champion immune-boosters. They attack free radicals that roam through the blood, seeking a cell wall they can latch onto and destroy. These vitamins, such as A, C, E, taken in the right doses, enter the bloodstream and attract those free radicals, attach to *them* and not your cells. Eventually, the radicals are carried out of your system.

Other vitamins, especially the B-complex family, give an incredible boost to various systems of your body. Stress, anxiety, consuming too much caffeine or alcohol can swiftly deplete your system of B vitamins. Replacing them can make a world of difference.

Before you launch into a vitamin regimen, though, check with your doctor, pharmacist, or a knowledgeable nutritionist. Read up, too! Don't just chuck vitamins down the hatch without knowing what you're doing! On the other hand, it's easier than you think, in this high-pressured world, to deplete your system.

Don't just settle for an "answer in a bottle," even though vitamins might really help. Think about other "boosters" you might add to your "regimen":

- Spend more time with friends who are "up," and with friends who can share healthy interests with you, whether an outdoor activity, a hobby, a community or service project, or a spiritual pursuit.
- How about getting back to a "joy" you left behind? Do you miss an old friend? Did you give up a hobby or pastime when you got married, had kids, or got caught up in your work? Get back to it—even if only occasionally.

Need a Boost? (continued)

- How much emotional "weight" are you carrying? Do you allow too many people to "unburden" their souls to you, so that they go away feeling lighter while you become depressed? Do you have constant burdens for the well-being of your children, parents, or siblings? Does your spouse feel free to spill his or her guts to you but rarely offers a listening, supportive ear? *Don't* set out on a crusade to change these folks—that will only add more weight, in the form of frustration. *Do* find some more friends who can listen and support and encourage you. These are people who will not try to fix your situation for you. Rather, they will offer encouragement, acceptance . . . and *fun!* . . . which you need.

- Keep your system "flushed" by regularly drinking plenty of pure water. Six to eight glasses a day is recommended!

- Keep that cardiovascular system in good working order with regular exercise, appropriate for your health status.

- Take regular walks in *safe* and scenic places. It's amazing what fresh air in the lungs will do. And it is amazing how taking in a long, panoramic view can lift your perspective from personal problems and, literally, restore a bigger view of life.

- Develop the attitude that "I am going to take charge of my well-being again." You don't need to exclude others or become selfish to value your own health.

member" it, surround it, and demolish it before trouble can start.

Do you see why having the strongest immune system possible is of prime importance? If your immune system is compromised, your shield against illness has been weakened. So in light of the recent discoveries about mood, emotion, and beliefs, and their effects on the immune system, how are we to respond?

If the mind is connected by nerve fibers to this wonderful defense "team," it is urgent to enlist the mind in support of the immune system. If you learn to tell yourself the truth, your healthy mind and emotions will strengthen your defenses against invading microbes, toxins, and cancerous cells.

The Mind, the Autonomic Nervous System, and the Chemicals We Make Ourselves

If you ever have headaches, backaches, or the feeling that you're "tight as a bowstring," you know about muscle tension. Or maybe you've felt the way anxiety can shift your heart into high-gear. But did you realize that all this activity in your body is mostly a response to what you are thinking? Talk about mind-body connections! All you have to do is scare yourself and the physical reactions begin. This kind of connection may be the most noticeable because of our discomfort when the autonomic nervous system revs up and creates a *tension* or *stress* response.

Then there are the neurotransmitters, hormones, and growth regulators labeled *neuropeptides*. These marvelous regulating juices course through us, bringing mood changes as well as governing various body functions. Amazingly, the receptors for many of the neurotransmitters cluster *in the intestines and in the brain*! When the biblical writers referred to the *bowels* as the seat of emotion, did they know intuitively that feelings, though controlled by the mind, are activated even in the intestines?[1]

And there is more. The cells of the immune system have receptors for some of these very same mood-changing neurotransmitters. So the astounding truth is this: *Your entire body is wired into a communication system centered in the brain—governed by the mind and the spirit!* As you ponder that fact, be sure to recognize one of its implications: Your health and your healing can be made better or worse by what you do with your mind! No wonder one of the leading researchers into mind-body connections has lost patience with those who insist on artificial divisions between psychology, immunology, and endocrinology! The fact is *there are no such divisions.* What actually happens in your body is more like a computer network than an assortment of "systems" operating independently.

A Whole New Discipline

Until a few years ago medical biologists insisted that the brain and the mind had nothing to do with the control of the immune system. The immune system was supposed to do its own "thinking," and its communications were a closed network in which the system talked only to various components within itself. But recent research by Candace Pert, chief of the section on brain biochemistry at the National Institute of Mental Health,[2] has turned this theory upside down and opened the way to a new discipline—whose title proclaims the power of the mind in relation to the immune system: *psycho-neuro-immunology.*

Very recently, newly discovered nerves were found to connect cells in the immune system *directly* to the hypothalamus, which connects directly to the brain. White blood cells of the immune system have now been shown to get messages from the same neurotransmitter chemicals that carry communication between nerve cells in the brain and the rest of the nervous system. Moreover, research on the neuropeptides has shown that these chemical messengers found in the brain are active all over the body. They can even be found in the intestines.(See endnote 2.) There is little room left to doubt that the immune system is under the direct control of your brain.

Your mind can render your natural "bodyguards" unable to do their work. On the other hand, disease-makers can be vanquished by an immune system propelled into full attack.

Does that mean that your brain can make you sick or well? It does if you consider that infection and cancer can show up as a result of suppression of your immune system.

Your mind can render your natural "bodyguards" unable to do their work. On the other hand, disease-makers can be vanquished by an immune system propelled into full attack. Because this is the case, you need to remember that what disturbs and distresses your mind *will* affect your brain. And what your brain does—especially what it does for a long time—*will* have mighty immune-system repercussions, positive or negative.

This is why a new model of health and illness has invited doctors to abandon the old biomedical model of simple materialism. That thinking led us to believe that eventually there will be a pill you can take for every illness. Rather, the spirit and the non-material mind will always influence the material brain and body, so that the body is to some extent the outward manifestation of the spirit and the mind. In fact, the spirit, mind, brain, nervous system, and the endocrine system make up a single complex network regulating our immune system. And all of these together affect our vulnerability to disease.

It would be too much to insist that the mind can cure every disease. Nevertheless, given the interconnections we can observe, it is likely that there is no such thing as a "purely physical problem"—or a problem beyond the reach of the mind. Especially when the human spirit is filled with the Spirit of truth.

To sum it all up: Among other causal factors, "Our health is controlled by our brain."[3] Let us add: "And our brain is controlled by our mind and spirit."

Now let's look at the ways in which faith empowers your spirit.

Notes

1. See, for example, Jeremiah 31:20 (KJV), where God says, "Is Ephraim my dear son? is he a pleasant child? for since I spake against him, I do earnestly remember him still: therefore my bowels are troubled for him; I will surely have mercy upon him, saith the LORD."
2. Justice, *Who Gets Sick*, p. 18. Says Pert, "The emotions are not just in the brain, they are in the body."
3. R. M. Restak

Chapter 6

Checking Your Spiritual "Diet"

The modern world tells us that *faith* is an outmoded relic from a pre-scientific dark age.

Has the need for faith really been replaced by medical technology—or is it possible that faith can accomplish what science cannot? Jesus told us that faith has the muscle to do what no power on earth can accomplish. With only a little faith, he said, you can move mountains into the sea. Those who take this literally and order chunks of the Rockies to fall into the Gulf of Mexico have been disappointed. Not only could they learn from the records that neither Jesus nor his most faithful followers ever tried such a thing, they could also learn from their failure that faith doesn't work that way. *Faith can do only what God wants to have done.* It is not a method for getting around God's will so you get your way instead.

What Kind of Mountains Does Faith Move?

When faith is firmly planted in God's will, it can move things that are as immovable as mountains. According to the Bible, faith enabled Abraham and Sarah to conceive a child at age 100 or so, and Joshua and the army of Israel to bring down the walls of a fortified city without touching them. According to Jesus, faith conquers fear, makes sick people well, and blind people see.

For you, faith can move mountains of hopelessness and discouragement. No technology on earth can give you hope or courage. But faith can.

There is always another virus waiting for us, always another cancer cell lurking inside threatening to get the upper hand. But faith helps us to rise up from within.

At one time I thought faith was a mysterious, complicated, ethereal thing that was only meant to save your soul from an eternity without God. I still believe living faith in Jesus Christ as Savior is necessary to receive God's free gift of salvation. But unfortunately for some, the word *faith* has picked up some ethereal—almost magical—overtones. This "mystification" narrows a person's concept of faith, shrinks it until it is some kind of power he can put to work for his own ends. And faith, to quote Martin Luther, is a "living, busy, active thing. . . ." It is meant to work first in the service of God, then in service of man.

Faith is not a simple way to get what you want from God. Please don't interpret anything in this book as teaching that "all you have to do is believe and you will be made completely whole."

On the other hand, true faith gives us the boldness to look honestly at our inborn cynicism, so we don't need to live our lives in skepticism, distrust, feelings of abandonment, anger, fear, and despair. Faith makes it possible to know that God is, and that he loves us and cares for us.

Yes, the world is full of dangers, and life has its risks. There is always another virus waiting for us, always another cancer cell lurking inside threatening to get the upper hand. But faith helps us to rise up from within, to know that no matter what happens in this life we will be raised one day as conquerors. And resting in the love of God this way, we improve our inward condition by crushing fear and doubt.

Faith Conquers

As I have said, this book is not about miracles. Miracles are not under our control, not statistically probable or predictable, nor can we explain them scientifically.

But the effect of faith, I have observed, is the benefit to physical health that comes from a firm, secure belief in God's goodness, no matter what the circumstances may be. This kind of inner calm, peace, happiness, and undefeatable attitude cannot fail to exercise a mighty power over the human body. Because the good things in life teach us that the Creator and Giver of life must be good, it is possible for anyone to believe *some* of these good things. But the person who knows the love of God can live a life illuminated by the light of faith. It is this full view of goodness and grace and positive outcomes that Jesus calls *the truth*. And the truth, he says, will set us free.[1] That is why, in many studies, people of faith do have, on the average, better physical (and mental) health than others.

But this matter of believing is not quite as simple as you might think. Let's look a little deeper.

Faith Is More Than . . .

The Greek word for *faith* that was used by the biblical authors means simply *believing*. That seems simple, at

"Spiritual Junk Food"

Some people throw away those unwanted catalogs that stuff our mailboxes before they even look at them. And for a very specific reason. Advertisers know they can bombard us with images of new clothes, trickier gadgets, prettier home furnishings, and the latest techno discoveries, and it will have an effect on us. It is called creating "strategic discontent." Seeing those tantalizing items on those slick pages makes us immediately compare them with our old nicked, frayed possessions . . . and whets our appetite for something *new*.

Are you consuming this kind of "spiritual junk food"? Are you constantly unhappy with what you own, or always wishing you had more? Then the advertisers have done a good job of clouding your inner being with discontent. No, it is not wrong to need or want the basics and certain material comforts. But if your hunger for consumer goods has begun to consume you it is time to rethink. And make a change.

The following is more spiritual junk food you need to eliminate from your "diet":

- music, films, books, and TV shows with negative and immoral content
- cynicism
- gossip
- a superior attitude . . . or a defeatist, inferior attitude
- too much time with escapist pastimes . . . too many evenings lost on who knows what.

Anything that fills time, but not your soul, may be clogging your spiritual arteries. Why not give it up and replace it with pastimes that build you in healthy ways?

first. But let's look at this more closely.

You could sit at a table and simply *identify* the food being served. "Yes, I truly believe that's bread. I know what that is—it's spinach. . . ." But this is not the same as eating a meal; believing in food won't nourish you.

Likewise, true faith has two aspects. It is possible to have a certain kind of belief that stops with merely identifying orthodox teachings. "Yes, I believe that Jesus really died on the cross. Yes, I believe the Bible is God's Word." That is doctrinal belief. The other aspect of faith is *using* what you know to be true—relying on God, trusting in him.

We need to ingest, and not merely identify spiritual food.

To do this you must actively tell yourself the truth. You must take it in and digest it—that is, let it fill your whole mind and confront inner pockets of fear, doubt, suspicion, blame, anger, resentment. It is confronting your own soul with the truth that if God *is* God I can trust him always, in all things. Fully "taking in" God's revelation of himself in this way will affect your mind, your emotions—and yes, your body too—in a positive way.

As long as we are talking about "ingesting" beliefs into our inner man, we have to look at the negative side of this.

When it comes to food, we don't thrive by indiscriminate eating. Nails, broomsticks, polyester fabrics, and ant poison may have important uses—but not in your diet. Taking in every negative statement about you, every fear-inducing news item, every irritating piece of gossip—this will have a toxic effect on you. Those sweet souls who soak up everything identified for them as "spiritual"—whether it comes from the pure stream of God's truth or from man-centered New Age spirituality—make a big mistake.

Here are truths that are centered in real Christian spirituality, ones that will have potent effects: God is not the universe itself, or even a life force in the universe; he is a transcendent Creator who is over all circumstances. God's will is good, never evil. God can strengthen you from within, even if all visible hope is gone. Like real food, *truthful* ideas are those that feed the soul with a healthful and true picture of reality.

What I am saying is this: Many people know the truth in their heads, but when problems arise they forget to actively put the truth into practice. You may think that God is good and in control, but what do you tell yourself when life gets tough, plans fail, finances get tight, or sickness strikes? Do you blame God? Or do you tell yourself, "Even in this, I'll wait for God to show me the good he can bring—whether my troubles vanish or not"?

You may think that God is good and in control, but what do you tell yourself when life gets tough, plans fail, finances get tight, or sickness strikes? Do you blame God?

The Power of Knowing the Truth

Joe Hallett is a wonderful example to all of us. Joe came to our Center for Christian Psychological Services in 1988 suffering from loneliness and despondency. His therapist, Psychologist-Pastor Steve Wiese, helped him to recognize that the cause of his anguish was not AIDS from which he'd suffered since 1986, nor the emptiness he'd once sought to heal with sex. Rather, Joe needed to replace the depressing distortions he was repeating to himself with disastrous results (three suicide attempts).

For Joe, the truth had long been distorted.

Ironically, he had committed his life to Christ Jesus and abandoned his former homosexual behavior eight months before any sign of sickness. After months as a new Christian, in spite of efforts to deny a growing problem, ugly symptoms of an opportunistic infection appeared.[2] "The glands in my neck were so swollen I looked like a bullfrog," was Joe's description of his severe lymphoma. His persistent cough had hung on for months and refused to respond to treatment. Joe admits now that he had a habit of repressing and denying facts that pointed to the obvious. "I never let myself consider that I might have AIDS. After all, I had been out of the gay lifestyle for eight months; I had rededicated myself to God. Surely he wouldn't let me ... No, it couldn't happen to me. Must be something else."

When Joe was given his military discharge physical in 1986, he got the bad news. "The doc wants you to call him," said his sergeant, staring at the ground. "Your blood test wasn't normal."

"I'm sorry, Joe," said the doctor. "You're HIV-positive." A supportive and compassionate man, the physician referred Joe to a counselor.

"I was in shock. Then I was angry," said Joe, "especially at God. I felt betrayed by him. Hadn't I given him everything? Hadn't I trusted him completely? Then I went into denial. My self-talk brimmed over with absurdity: 'The test must have been mistaken. I'm not going to die. They'll find out I don't have the virus after all.' Next I tried bargaining with God. That was a failure before it started. What did I have to bargain with? I'd already given up the gay lifestyle, my search for happiness, everything. I had no bargaining chips left. And now they were telling me I had, perhaps, two years to live.

" 'Stay in the army,' I told myself at first. 'You're going to die anyway. Let them take care of you.' But I thought it over and concluded that the best place to spend my last two years was probably not the army," Joe mused.

" 'Go home to your folks, and let them take care of you,' I told myself. So I tried living with my parents for four to five months. But we just couldn't talk about important things I needed to talk about."

Joe then moved to Minneapolis where he found a group of Christian ex-gays in an organization called *Outpost*—people he could talk with to find encouragement. "But now I warned myself, 'Don't join *Outpost*. You're dying of AIDS. Outpost is not for you.' " He joined anyway.

"Then I found a house I wanted to buy and counseled myself, 'Don't buy a house. You're dying of AIDS, and you don't need the stress.' I bought it anyway. Then I planned a garden. Again, my thoughts wanted to paralyze me. 'Don't start a garden. Digging in the dirt wouldn't be good for you. You're dying of AIDS.' But I did it anyway—and now I enjoy a garden full of tulips, hyacinths, strawberries, raspberries, and blueberries. I got some cats, and my self-talk filled with more negatives. 'Don't, you'll be allergic.' But I have three cats and they're not killing me. And a year ago I got married with a chorus of inner voices warning me against doing that, too."

What a pattern! Joe not only told himself the truth to counter his own negative, deceptive self-talk, he acted in obedience to a fundamental *truth*—namely, that his life is in the hands of a God who has said, "I am the Lord who heals you." Because of right thinking and acting, Joe has survived for ten years after receiving his two-year sentence. Why? Because Joe *tells* himself the truth and *lives* by it. He finds encouragement in God and support in his wife and friends—all of whom encourage him and help him to live by insisting on the truth.

Following are Joe's life-sustaining truths. According to

him, these truths keep him going. Joe tells himself:

- *Take risks.* I must make myself take risks, trusting God to see me through. Had I not taken risks and made decisions I was afraid to make, I believe I would not be alive.
- *Pursue God.* When other goals look alluring, I remind myself that only one thing is needful: Jesus himself, my God and my Savior.
- *Choose life.* I know I can, to a certain extent, choose life. When I let go, when I tell myself life is not worth living, I get sick. When I have a heavy schedule of speaking and ministering to others, believing life is in part mine for the choosing, I get better.
- *Rest in God's goodness.* I tell myself God *wants* me to have a good life every day, and I believe God's own self-talk as it is revealed in Jeremiah 29:11: " 'I know the plans I have for you,' declares the LORD, 'plans to prosper you and not to harm you, plans to give you hope and a future.' " So I treat every single day of life as a gift, precious because it comes from God.
- *Humor helps.* I laugh at life's contradictions and absurdities and this keeps me much healthier than getting upset at them.
- *Hope and dream.* Living "one day at a time" is not enough for me. I need hopes and dreams. If God has a plan for me, I need to try to get with the plan. And I sense that God wants me to dream and plan according to his will as I understand it. I sense God saying, "Go for it, Joe!"

This kind of faith is spiritual in the highest sense, drawing on truths about God, *and* it is practical and down to earth as well. Joe's faith—his determined effort to replace defeating self-talk with positive, life-giving truth—has literally kept him alive. Joe has no idea how much

longer he will live. Nor does faith give him—or any of us—
iron-clad guarantees. But Joe's faith helps him live every
day to the fullest.

What is your spiritual "diet" like? What do you feed
your soul every day? Is it the spiritual diet of an "over-
comer" or the soul food of a defeatist?

Think it over.

Seriously.

Notes

1. John 8:31–36
2. As the immune system breaks down in persons with
   AIDS, infectious organisms take advantage of the "opportunity" to wreak havoc. An *opportunistic infection* is an
   infection by a microorganism that normally does not
   cause disease but becomes pathogenic when the body's
   immune system is impaired and unable to fight off infection, as in AIDS and certain other diseases.

Chapter 7

Present Tense

Have you ever taken the time to consider what causes you to feel stressed? How *much* stress do you carry at any given time? What is your stress level?

Hidden Stress and Your Health

Many people define stress as the *events* that threaten us or make heavy demands on us and make us upset. If that's what you believe *stress* is, get ready for the new facts.

Stress is not *something that happens to us*, but stress is *the way we respond to what happens*. When some event occurs *and we perceive the situation to be beyond our ability to handle it*, that is stress. What we tell ourselves about the event is what makes an event stressful.

Take an example discussed by Dr. Walter B. Cannon, the Harvard physiologist who invented the well-known term for stress reactions—*the fight or flight response*. Cannon recounted this incident:

A youth on a journey stayed overnight at the home of a friend. For breakfast, the older friend served wild hen, a food the young in that culture were forbidden to eat under threat of dire consequences. When the young man asked if the meat was by chance wild hen, his friend lied, "No!" So the youth ate and went on his way, feeling fine. Years later the two met by chance and the older man laughingly recounted how he had tricked the other into eating the forbidden food. The younger man became terribly frightened, began to shake and tremble, and within twenty-four hours was dead! His stress, so severe as to be fatal, was entirely a matter of his perception of the situation.[1]

Immobilized by Perceptions

Let me tell you about Marvin who wrote to me on the Internet to tell me of his experience. An accident had laid him up for more than a year, Marvin wrote, "and I thought I was going to be a total invalid. But then I turned to the Word of God and I read that the Lord is my strength.[2] I decided that I didn't need to remain impaired. I got up and forged painfully ahead, moving forward step by step."

Though Marvin's initial perception actually crippled him, he took God's Word seriously and soon returned to work. He learned that the stress was not a result of his physical injury alone but, more devastatingly, his *perception* that the situation was beyond his ability to cope.

Most individual cases of remarkable physical response to mental and emotional changes do not occur in the context of controlled scientific studies. Therefore, they do not make it into scientific publications. Yet every physician has witnessed these turnarounds. Dr. Andrew Weil[3] tells of a "bank president with chronic hypertension, whose blood pressure normalized one day after his wife filed for divorce. It dropped to 120/80 and stayed there." This does not suggest that divorce is "the answer" to stressful marriages, or that it is a good thing, but in this man's case the sign that a stressful relationship would end resulted in physical improvement. Dr. Weil also notes that he has seen serious medical problems resolve themselves when people fall in love. His point is that the mind and emotions often have the power to heal the body. Many doctors have observed, as I have, that if a patient becomes aware of anger and expresses it, this sometimes results in a turn for the better.

Most individual cases of remarkable physical response to mental and emotional changes do not occur in the context of controlled scientific studies. Therefore, they do not make it into scientific publications. Yet every physician has witnessed these turnarounds.

What Makes the Difference Among the Cadets?

Stanislav Kasl and his colleagues at Yale's department of epidemiology noticed that 194 West Point cadets out of a class of 1400 contracted Epstein-Barr virus over four years at the school. But only 48 became more severely ill with mono. Kasl and his co-workers found a significant difference. Most of the seriously ill cadets had fathers who imparted to their sons an extreme need to achieve in order to be worthwhile. These young men, believing they absolutely had to perform at top level, were in a tough spot

True or False Stress Test

Some of us are "stress-aholics" and imagine that we are thriving on stress and constant pressure or chaos. True, pressure can trigger a shot of adrenaline for the short-haul, but when the craziness is over we're quite depleted. Others of us get by telling ourselves that stress isn't really affecting us. (Those chest pains are just gas! That chronic indigestion must be something we ate!)

In effect, we accept stress as a *lifestyle*—and even encourage it in our children! Moving through life with a relaxed attitude seems somehow wrong, or at least unrealistic. What are your answers to these "true"/"false" questions? (Key at the bottom.)

I will be able to relax and enjoy life when:

T	F	my financial pressures are over.
T	F	my health improves.
T	F	someone I love has resolved their problems.
T	F	I meet the "right" man/woman
T	F	I get the "right" job, title, or salary.
T	F	someone who has hurt me says they are sorry.
T	F	my children are settled in their lives.
T	F	I am relieved of responsibilities I never asked for.
T	F	certain people just leave me alone to do my own thing and live life my way.

(**Key:** This is a trick test! Yes, people and circumstances can bring pressure to bear on us. But outward circumstances don't *have* to keep us stressed-out. You can build healthy stress-relievers into your daily life. Likewise, eliminating obvious stress factors will not *necessarily* change your life if you are a virtual "stress battery" who stores up tension. Stop looking only at the people and circumstances, and begin to take charge of the de-stressing you need, by learning healthier inner life habits.)

when their grades were below average. Cadets who had Epstein-Barr but *never developed mononucleosis* had less need to excel and make top grades. The researchers found among the 48 that the *pressure* created by their own perceptions kept them in a state of constant anxiety, which in turn led to a depressed immune response. It was how these students perceived themselves that made the difference!

Not Conflicts and Demands, But How We Handle Them . . .

Numerous medical researchers have made the link between the way we perceive our situation and our susceptibility to sickness. At Cornell Medical College in New York, researchers compared telephone operators who were frequently ill with others on the same job who were hardly ever sick. The sickness-prone operators tended to be dissatisfied and discontented with their situation. What made the difference in their physical health was the way they *perceived* common life difficulties such as family conflicts or too many demands from other people.[4]

Dr. Blair Justice has described many experiments leading to similar conclusions. "No one factor determines who gets sick. A key cofactor is the cognitive. Thinking (nonmaterial and intangible) is perfectly capable of affecting the physical (tangible) world—our bodies."[5] According to Dr. Justice, stress is not caused by events in the environment, but what we tell ourselves about events in the environment. Whether events happening around us make us sick depends on how we view our troubles and what chemical messengers we trigger in our brains.

Those who have long believed that stress consists of changes happening *to* us, rather than our *reaction* to changes, will have to adjust their thinking because the meaning of the word has been changing recently. More and more experts on stress are beginning to use the word to mean an individual's attitude and interpretation of situations, not the situations themselves.

Getting a handle on stress is one of the most powerful things you can do to create an inner climate conducive to better health.

———

Throughout the rest of this book we'll develop a clear plan to de-stress your inner spirit—a plan that I hope will work for you.

Notes

1. Herbert Benson, M.D., *The Mind-Body Effect* (New York: Simon & Schuster, 1979), pp. 22ff.
2. This fascinating truth that strength itself is not altogether a matter of the physical equipment either of body or of tools one has available, but that strength is spiritual and is to be found in God is repeated numerous times in the Bible. It is time we renewed our own strength through calling up this truth! The passage Marvin saw could well have been Psalm 28:7–8 (KJV), "The LORD is my strength and my shield; my heart trusted in him, and I am helped: therefore my heart greatly rejoiceth; and with my song will I praise him. The LORD is their strength, and he is the saving strength of his anointed."
3. Andrew Weil, M.D., *Spontaneous Healing* (New York: Alfred A. Knopf, 1995), pp. 98–99.
4. L. E. Hinkle and H. G. Wolff, "Ecological investigations of the relationship between illness, life experiences, and the social environment," *Annals of Internal Medicine* (1958): 49, 1373–88.
5. Blair Justice, Ph.D., *Who Gets Sick: How Beliefs, Moods, and Thoughts Affect Your Health* (Los Angeles: Jeremy P. Tarcher, Inc. and Houston: Peak Press, 1988). Distributed by St. Martin's Press, New York.

Chapter 8

The Truth About "Bad News"

People who receive a diagnosis of cancer, hepatitis, or heart disease usually have one thought: "I'm going to die from this!"

I believe this is the result of cultural training. Our culture has trained us to think there are certain diagnoses that amount to a death sentence. Never is it as sure and hopeless as that. There are many things you can do to increase your well-being and chances of survival.

Scientific investigators have amassed data, showing that certain approaches are definitely effective against even the most frightening diseases.

Jason's Victory

Eight-year-old Jason Gaes of Worthington, Minnesota, was diagnosed with Burkitt's lymphoma, a cancer so unusual only a few children have it. Jason's parents learned their son had only one chance in five of surviving. Yet months later, on June 28, 1986, a crowd of more than 500 friends and relatives thronged to Jason's home for his victory party—and later attended his church, which held a special service of thanksgiving to God. Had you been one of the fortunate guests at his celebration, you would have seen Jason greeting his guests in a tux—for he had *fully recovered!*

If you like, you can read the book Jason wrote, *My Book for Kids With Cansur.* About his book, Jason writes, "The rezin I wanted to write a book about having cansur is because every book I read about kids with cansur they always die. I want to tell you kids don't always die. If you get cansur don't be scared cause lots of people get over having cansur and grow up without dying."[1]

As Jason describes his hospitalization and treatment, he comments that having "cansur" is not all bad. Then he describes the things that are fun about the experience, as well as those things that can be painful, like chemotherapy.

Jason's experience demonstrates the possibility of giving even the most frightening diseases a fight that ends in victory.

Strong in Heart

Even people with severe illnesses can stoke up their body's efforts to repair.

"My brother, Donald, had cancer and he learned how to increase his survival time sixfold!" said an acquaintance, Sister Anita Germain, CSJ, when I told her I was researching the power of the human mind and spirit to facilitate physical healing. Donald was forty-six when he learned that *single-cell carcinoma* had taken root in his lung with metastases spreading to his liver and lymph nodes. Neither surgery nor radiation would be effective. His doctor shook his head. "Three months is all the time you have. Set your life in order."

But Donald was a man of prayer who knew his times were in God's hands.

"My brother was the family member who even when our family went camping would kneel beside his sleeping bag and pray every night with a heart full of thanksgiving, peace, and joy," said Anita.

Special healing prayer with laying-on of hands was ministered by a Christian woman. "My brother felt a power coursing through him and the warmth of love in his lungs and throughout his body," Anita recalled. "It was the power of God." Alongside the powerful prayer was Donald's steadfast belief. He and his family and friends joined together in believing that no statistical prediction could determine a life-span, and that the healing work to be done by his spirit, mind, and body had been blessed by God.

The result was that nine months later—when he was supposed to have been long-dead, Donald was still working energetically at his job as maintenance supervisor for a high school. And he was still praying and praising God for every day of life. Eventually, the cancer took over—but by then Donald had lengthened his life by *six times the doctor's prognosis*.

The Value of Laughter

Scientific studies on the mind-body connection have proved that laughter is a strong immune booster, right along with a positive mental attitude.

Norman Cousins' astonishing experience shows how laughter can be great medicine. In his book *Anatomy of an Illness as Perceived by the Patient: Reflections on Healing and Regeneration*, Mr. Cousins wrote to make a point: The patient can and must take an active role in the treatment of

Get "Well" Versed

You *can* re-season your innermost being! It means replacing doubtful, hopeless, negative, and distrustful attitudes embedded in your spirit with real, activated trust. Nothing can fill you with a sense of well-being like God's Word.

Take some time each day to be alone, and bring the truth of God's Word into contact with your deepest inner needs, questions, pains, fears, and disappointments. (Don't bother trying to hide them from God with a fake smile and chirpy pretense—he sees your heart more clearly than you do!) Try personalizing these verses:

"I will trust in your unfailing love [when] _____" (Psalm 13:5).

"I lift up my soul; in you I trust [and I do not trust in] _____" (Psalm 25:2).

"I will trust in the Lord and do good [when anger and vengeful impulses tempt me to do bad to] _____" (Psalm 37:3).

"Trust in him and he will do this _____" (Psalm 37:5).

"In God I trust and will not be afraid [of] _____" (Psalm 56:4).

No doubt you picked up on a theme here. How is your attitude of trust in the Lord?

illness. The results of such self-care are wonderful. Cousins had become seriously ill with ankylosing spondylitis, a serious collagen disease that offered him only a one in 500 chance of full recovery.

Had Cousins taken those odds as the predictor of his future, he would have planned his funeral. Instead, he got together with his physician to consider his situation. After careful thought, they determined that his illness came about after his immune system had been severely stressed on a recent and difficult overseas journey. They concluded that the underlying cause of his illness was adrenal exhaustion.

Cousins began studying the available literature. He learned that full functioning of the adrenal glands is essential for combating illness. He also found that adrenal exhaustion can result from emotional tension, frustration, and chronic anger. And he came to realize that negative emotions are the result of negative, untruthful root beliefs—beliefs that create an inner climate of hopelessness, despair, and resentment. *Was it possible,* he asked himself, *that love, hope, faith, laughter, confidence, and the will to live might cause positive chemical and hormonal changes? Could such changes of mind and emotion bring health?*

After careful study, Mr. Cousins concluded that he could not be helped by taking more pain medication and that hospital nutrition and routines were counterproductive for his particular needs. He and his doctor formulated a new kind of treatment program—with laughter as the chief ingredient! For Cousins, it was easy enough to have hope and love and faith. But generating laughter would take some doing. He obtained some old Marx brothers films, and dozens of video episodes of a current TV comedy, *Candid Camera.*

It worked.

"Ten minutes of genuine belly laughter had an anesthetic effect and would give me at least two hours of pain-free sleep," Cousins wrote. Reading from the works of some of the best humorists supplemented the films. The healthful effects of all were scientifically documented. Cousins' blood sedimentation rates dropped after each laughter episode, and the effect not only lasted but built over time.

Cousins next added to his self-devised regimen large doses of vitamin C infused intravenously. His sed rate dropped at an even faster rate, his fever receded, and his pulse no longer raced. Completely off drugs and sleeping pills, he enjoyed increasingly long periods of natural sleep.

Mr. Cousins and his doctor formulated a new kind of treatment program—with laughter as the chief ingredient!

Eventually his symptoms abated enough that Cousins was able to return to work as editor of the *Saturday Review*. That was miracle enough!

Here is Norman Cousins' summary of his recovery:

> Year by year the mobility has improved. I have become pain-free except for one shoulder and my knees. . . . I hit a tennis ball or golf ball. . . . I can ride a horse flat out, and hold a camera with a steady hand. And I have recaptured my ambition to play Bach's *Toccata and Fugue in D-minor*, though I find the going slower and tougher than I had hoped. My neck has a full turning radius again despite the statement of specialists . . . that I would have to adjust to a quarter turn.[2]

Cousins' valuable conclusions from his experience—which have since been confirmed—can help us all. First, the will to live makes all the difference because will affects physiological reality. The will to live has biochemical and physical correlates that have healing power. Second, the capacity of the human body to regenerate is fantastic—even when the prospects are bleak. Third, Mr. Cousins, working with his physician, took responsibility for his own treatment rather than wait passively for the doctors to make him well.

More Than a "Positive Attitude"

Never in his remarkable book does Cousins attribute his healing to the blessing of God. He apparently thought that somehow the finite human person has all that is needed to thrive and survive if only he will use it. Cousins made use of some positive thoughts and attitudes—but he could have gone on to discover a spiritual new birth, into a life that has no end. In Christ he could have found an eternal well of joy that never runs dry. Mr. Cousins seems to have cut his journey short just at the threshold of the greatest and most positive truth of all—that true healing is knowing Christ, no matter what our outer circumstances bring.

It may be the reverse for you. You may know the most significant truth of all—that Christ is Lord—but perhaps you have not learned to exercise eternal hope and inner joy for the benefit of your health. The news is very good and the future is hopeful!

Let's get down to business now and look at the ways *you* can make this great new information work for you.

Notes

1. Jason Gaes, *My Book for Kids With Cansur* (Aberdeen, S.D.: Melios & Peterson Publishing, Inc., 1987).
2. Norman Cousins, *Anatomy of an Illness As Perceived by the Patient* (New York: Norton, 1979; New York: Bantam, 1981).

Chapter 9

What *Do* You Believe?

"Now may the God of peace Himself sanctify you completely; and may your whole spirit, soul, and body be preserved blameless at the coming of our Lord Jesus Christ" (1 Thessalonians 5:23, NKJV).

When the apostle Paul wrote these words to believers in a young church, he seems to have understood that the power of a sound mind can be used by God to help you become robust and healthy in body. According to several research studies,[1] the mind, informed by positive thoughts, can do just that among practicing Christian believers. We have seen examples demonstrating how the connection between mind and body can be used to make you sick and how it can be used to make you well.

Why and *how* do your beliefs make a difference in matters of health? As we've seen, beliefs and thoughts create your inner state and your emotions. Your inner state is a major force that influences your immune system.

Counseling Helps Sick People Heal

Two psychologists, Dr. Ronald Grossath-Maticek at the University of Heidelberg in Germany, and his collaborator Dr. Hans Eysenck, found that they could alter death rates from cancer and heart disease with the use of *counseling*.[2] Many other scientific investigations have established that counseling seriously ill people, teaching them how to replace disease-generating thoughts with health-giving truth, can nearly double their survival time. Furthermore, these studies show that *positive, hopeful, encouraging* beliefs make people better—while a steady "diet" of negative, bitter, and fearful thoughts make them sick. Such thoughts are like poison to the body's healing systems.

Scientific investigations have established that counseling seriously ill people, teaching them how to replace disease-generating thoughts with health-giving truth, can nearly double their survival time.

Pathological Beliefs and Thoughts

Let's look at some specific health-destroying beliefs that psychologists and researchers have discovered:

- Life is hopeless.
- I must not let myself face and feel negative emotions—they're too painful and may overwhelm me.
- I am a helpless victim—life and all its circumstances are in charge of what happens to me.
- If I get a serious illness, the worst will happen and I will die.

- Medical treatments hardly ever work, and they have awful, unbearable side-effects.
- Once you have a disease, there is nothing you can do to help yourself.
- I'd like to be positive and hopeful—but I *can't help* being hopeless and depressed. It's these circumstances. . . .
- There is nothing I can do to change my negative beliefs, even though I know they are upsetting me and making me worse.
- I'm only going to get worse, and then I'll be nothing but a burden to everybody.
- Even if I get well I can't prevent a relapse. And I can't live with this out-of-control feeling.
- I might be all right now, but I don't know how to protect myself—or someone I love—from getting a dreadful illness.

Pathogenic Thoughts Are *Misrepresentations*

Are your beliefs founded in these hope-destroying ideas? If so, they may not appear to you to be misrepresentations of the truth; they may appear to be statements about reality. But they are devoid of *spiritual* reality and so they lack hope. As such, they can drain you of life from the inside out, weakening the natural health-producing functions God has built into your body for healing. The truly good news is that they *can* be changed. You can renew your mind, as the Bible suggests (see Romans 12:1–2).

Some readers will recognize this list of destructive fallacies as the sort of mental baggage I have labeled *misbeliefs* in previous writing. I borrowed this term from Martin Luther, who used it to describe the kind of lies the devil plants in our minds to defeat us spiritually. What I have never written about before is the assault on our *physical* health that comes when our mind and spirit are enslaved by defeated thinking.

Changing Unhealthy Thoughts

Doctors and counselors working in the new medical field of mind-body healing—*psychoneuroimmunology*—know that a major part of their work consists of helping people change their minds. Counselors have discovered that they can help people—especially those who know the Lord Jesus Christ as their Light and Life—recover, and live longer, if they replace

- *despair and giving up* with *resolve and the will to get well;*
- *hopelessness* with *optimism;*
- *helplessness and a sense of abandonment* with *trust in the care and power of God.*

If you are concerned about your health or have a serious disease, it's important to take an inventory of your innermost beliefs. Just before we examine some commonly held negative beliefs, let's establish some guidelines.

C. Maxwell Maultsby, Jr., a therapist who has written much about the power of our beliefs, has offered five questions for testing the validity of a belief. I have altered Maultsby's questions somewhat to suit our particular purpose. You can use them to check your own illness-health beliefs. Ask yourself:

1. *Is this belief factually correct according to the evidence, including Scripture?*
2. *Will this belief help me protect myself against self-inflicted misery and illness?*
3. *Will this belief help me reach my goals in the short-term and in the long-range?*

4. *Will this belief help me remain in harmony and at peace with God and, as much as possible, with other people?*

5. *Will this belief help me maintain the emotions I want to feel?*

To see how these questions work, let's apply them to a belief often held by people with a major illness: *I can't help myself—this illness is bigger than I am.*

1. *Is this belief factually correct?* No. It is dead wrong. The illness is not bigger than you are, because you are a person made in the image of God. There is much you can do to help yourself.

2. *Will this belief help me protect myself?* Not at all. Telling yourself you are beaten before you start is precisely what every man in the Israelite army did when they were challenged by the giant Goliath. The Israelites were stymied without a fight! Then a mere boy, David, showed up with a strong belief in God and proved that nobody needs to declare himself beaten before he starts. This fatal false belief will keep you from even trying to beat your illness.

3. *Will this belief help me to reach my goals in the short-term and in the long-range?* No way! It will help you reach none of them. Yes, it might give you a certain short-term feeling of relief as it releases you from having to make an effort. But in the long-run, it reduces your chances of winning by taking you out of the race.

4. *Will this belief help me remain in harmony and at peace with God and with other people?* This belief could cause you to withdraw from relationships, causing you simply to give up.

5. *Will this belief help me maintain the emotions I want to feel?* Not by a long shot! This belief will lead to depression, hopelessness, and despair—some of the most painful emotions human beings suffer.

Ask yourself these questions in relation to your own beliefs about your illness. Remember this crucial set of facts:

Your beliefs create your thoughts.
Your thoughts generate feelings.
Your feelings affect your body's healing systems.

What you believe and tell yourself can become a powerful medication in your personal pharmacy!

Secrets Revealed by Those Who Have Recovered

Some who have recovered from threatening diseases have revealed their secrets. The inner climate they created sounds very different from the dark pronouncements of those who make themselves worse. Here are some examples of beliefs others have found healing:

- I refuse to believe my diagnosis is a death sentence.
- I believe God is on the side of my healing because his unbreakable Word says so.
- I believe treatment is effective against this illness, especially the skillful efforts of scientific medicine *combined* with my strategies for replacing lying thoughts with truth.
- I believe my hormones and immune system are on the side of my healing and are even now working to overcome this illness.
- I believe I am personally responsible for my treatment and for managing it.
- I believe hope is a choice. I choose hope, not hopelessness.
- My major aim is to have a mind fully submitted to the Spirit of God and his truth, not just to see better lab results or improvement in physical symptoms.

- I believe I am on earth to share Christ, hope, and joy with others. I am here only to love others, regardless of my physical condition.
- I believe that God's will is good. I believe that he loves me and wants only the best for me—whatever he is allowing me to experience right now.
- I can recover from this illness and live a rich, productive life of service. But whether I recover or not, I am going to leave this life someday regardless. Until then I can live a full life of service every day for as long as I am given.

Testing the Beliefs of Those Who Get Better

Now let's apply the five test questions to one of the beliefs of people who succeed in winning even in the face of serious illness. Let's take *"I believe hope is a choice."*

1. *Is this belief factually correct according to the evidence, including Scripture?* Yes. See, for instance, the imperative in Psalm 42:5, NKJV: "Why are you cast down, O my soul? And why are you disquieted within me? Hope in God, for I shall yet praise Him for the help of His countenance." God would not tell you to hope in him if you couldn't choose to do it. Furthermore, the testimonies of others show how we can determine that we are going to do battle against hopelessness and win.

2. *Will this belief help me protect myself against self-inflicted misery and illness?* When your mind is full of hope, hope will protect your emotions and fight your sickness. God's Word says that the hope produced in the midst of suffering does not disappoint us.[3] That is, it works and bears fruit! And doesn't common sense tell you that the person whose heart is fixed upon hope will from it produce more positive, healing emotions and less self-inflicted misery?

3. *Will this belief help me reach my goals in the short-term and in the long-range?* Certainly, because your goals include peace of mind and heart, emotional and physical improvement, and recovery.

4. *Will this belief help me remain at peace with God and, as much as possible, with other people?* Yes. A mind full of hope and the positive beliefs associated with it will not alienate God by blaming him or alienate others with self-pity.

5. *Will this belief help me maintain the emotions I want to feel?* Of course. People who have determined to hope feel less depressed, more optimistic, less anxious, more confident, more upbeat.

Starting Your Own Notebook of Healing

You can see from our examples how this works. Why not begin to help yourself by writing your own "Conquering Illness Notebook"? Give it a title of your own, including your name or the name of your sickness. For instance, "Pete's Conquering Arthritis Notebook," or "Rita's Journey Toward Good Health."

You may want to write an introduction that includes something about your life and your goals. After that, begin by listing your unwanted thoughts. Tap into your thinking processes when you are feeling fear or discouragement and jot down the negative thoughts that come to mind. When you have listed eight or ten of them, test them with the five questions in this chapter. Be sure to write all this out in your notebook. After that, try formulating the upbeat, positive thoughts with which you intend to replace your misbeliefs and write them down. Finally, test these new thoughts with each of the five questions and write out the results.

All this may take several pages. Take all the time and

space you need. This is an important step. From it, you will be able to begin to fashion a program to promote an attitude of health and well-being at the core of your spirit. *Go to it!*

Notes

1. Some of these studies are listed here for reference: B. Spilka and D. McIntosh, "Religion and Physical Health: the Role of Personal Faith and Control Beliefs," *Research in the Social Scientific Study of Religion* (1990): 2, 167–194; D. M. Zuckerman, S. V. Kasl, and A. M. Ostfield, "Psychological predictors of mortality among the elderly poor," *American Journal of Epidemiology* (1984): 119, 410–423; G. W. Comstock and K. B. Partridge, "Church attendance and health," *Journal of Chronic Disease* (1972): 25, 665–672.
2. O. Carl Simonton, M.D., and Reid M. Henson, with Brenda Hampton, *The Healing Journey* (New York: Bantam, 1992), p. 9.
3. Romans 5:3–5, RSV. More than that, we rejoice in our sufferings, knowing that suffering produces endurance, and endurance produces character, and character produces hope, *and hope does not disappoint us*, because God's love has been poured into our hearts through the Holy Spirit which has been given to us (emphasis added).

Chapter 10

The Prayer Connection

So far we've looked mainly at the role our thoughts play in healing and disease. Of course, both healing and disease have multiple causes and therefore getting better involves doing a number of things as well as we can. Fellowship, exercise, nutrition, rest, and spiritual communion all make a difference. Changing our thoughts must not be separated from these other efforts.

Communing with God in prayer, for example, is one of the most important things we can do.

Herb Mjorud's story can show us how to add prayer—along with sensible medical treatment—to the healing regime. Mjorud, a pastor, was diagnosed with lymphoma in 1980. This tumor was not the first bout in his epic struggle with cancer. Four previous episodes ended with remissions, sometimes dramatic healings in response to prayer, sometimes in response to surgery and chemotherapy. This time the cancer had metastasized so that its malignant cells had migrated and taken root all through his body. The tumor was seeding little copies of itself everywhere. That this man who had prayed so powerfully for the healing of others would himself have a terminal disease struck those of us who knew him as ironic. Many of his friends said, "Wouldn't you think that he of all people would have a kind of spiritual immunity?"

That a man who had prayed so powerfully for the healing of others would himself have a terminal disease struck those of us who knew him as ironic.

A Demonstration of Standing Firm in Truth

Mjorud filled his mind with the truth about God's healing power. Along with many brothers and sisters in Christ, he prayed fervently for his complete healing. Still, nothing changed for the better. The cancer only progressed. After months, it appeared certain that chemotherapy with all its rigors was not arresting tumor growth. He was dying.

Some Christians believe that God never speaks to people today. I believe he does. Several of the people whose stories I researched for this book tell of their conversations with God. Herbert Mjorud is one of those. He wrote to me that at this moment of discouragement God spoke to him. The words resounded through his thoughts loud and clear, and with loving authority: *Spend three days in prayer and praise, and on the third day I will do something.*

Mjorud had little doubt that he heard the Lord. But how could he praise God? Herb was so weak he couldn't speak, let alone sing hymns of praise. Besides, the chemotherapy had utterly destroyed his voice. So for three days, hour after hour, he listened to a favorite worship album over and over, using the voices of the singers as his own.

On the third day Mjorud, at the brink of death, again heard the voice of the Lord in prayer. This time the command was even stronger. *Do what I did to the fig tree. Read Mark 11.*

Herb knew the story. Jesus had cursed a fruitless tree and consequently it died. Suddenly Herb believed that God himself had revealed his will—and that the tumor was going to wither and die, too. Whispering, he thanked God for cursing the tumor down to its roots.

Remarkably, Herb's voice returned immediately and in full force—and so did his appetite. He ate ravenously.

Days later when the oncologist examined him and tested his blood, he could say only, "There is no cancer. Without doubt you have had a miracle."

Oddly, this is not the end of the story. In the spring of 1981 Mjorud was again hit with a hard bout of cancer—this time with another long and arduous operation. Again this pastor who had seen the Lord rescue him four times was sent home to die. He couldn't eat. He could only pray. And he stood firmly believing that God had again spoken to him, saying, *I will restore you to health and heal your wounds.*[1] Once more—against all odds, contrary to the predictions of medical experts—Mjorud's health was fully restored!

Today, after eight bouts with cancer, he has been free of illness for fourteen years.[2]

It would have been an easy matter to become discouraged, hopeless, and depressed, especially when five return bouts of cancer indicated that the disease was winning. If God's healing was real, wouldn't he have done the job perfectly, once and for all? Mjorud did not allow himself to

dwell on discouraging negatives. Instead, the positive fact
Evangelist Mjorud kept telling himself was this: God has
said he will heal you and he doesn't lie. God cannot go
back on his promise. He *must* heal you if you are to be
healed at all. This man did not avoid medical treatment,
but he never forgot one thing: No matter how good your
physician, no matter how conscientious the nurses and relatives who care for you, only God's blessing can heal. And
an upbeat, positive, fact-based attitude is one of his instruments.

An Internist Looks at the Records

Prayer is an important instrument in opening the way
to God's healing because it can bring new convictions and
change your mind-set. Sometimes the spotlight appears to
be on keeping up a constant verbal harangue at God, as if
trying to pump up a "positive confession" will "release"
healing power. The truth is, God must clearly reveal his
will in a given situation. And when he gives the inner conviction that healing is his will, healing *will* come as we rest
and relax and rejoice that his power is at work in us.

Unfortunately, most healings through prayer have not
been rigorously studied by medical researchers. Only occasionally have healings attributable to prayer been medically documented. Here is a list of people healed of seemingly incurable ailments. As you run through the list, pay
attention to the diagnoses:

> *Lisa Larios*—reticulum cell sarcoma of the right pelvic
> bone.
> *Elfrieda Stauffer*—chronic rheumatoid arthritis with
> severe disability.
> *Marie Rosenberger*—malignant brain tumor(*glioma*) of
> the left temporal lobe.

Marvin Bird—arteriosclerotic heart disease.

Each of these people was healed in response to prayer. In a remarkable book entitled *The Miracles*, a physician with a degree qualifying him for research in medicine published his findings in these and six other cases. H. Richard Casdorph, M.D., Ph.D., assembled all the available medical records for ten patients who were dramatically healed in response to prayer, carefully documenting their pathologies and diagnoses, including medical tests and X rays, and spelling out the medical findings on these same patients after their healings. True, many other stories about remarkable recoveries have been published, but for the most part they make no attempt to provide hard convincing evidence that divine healings actually occurred. Few skeptics will be impressed with what is scornfully called "mere anecdotal evidence." This is why Casdorph's work was needed. Having access to scientifically documented evidence offers another kind of testimony to the truth that prayer does lead to healing. Casdorph's interesting little book constitutes clear medical evidence that God heals in response to prayer, even in cases where there was virtually no chance of recovery.[3]

An Incredible Demonstration

Like Casdorph, cardiologist Randolph Byrd set up a prayer experiment. He wanted to isolate the effects of prayer for sick persons from the possibility that healing effects could be attributed to such things as the power of suggestion and the positive effects of the touch of caring hands.

Dr. Byrd set up the experiment so that the Christians who agreed to pray for patients never saw or contacted the people they prayed for. Furthermore, neither the patients

A Much More Difficult Exercise

In weight-lifting, the idea is to build your muscles over a period of time by gradually hoisting more and more weight. Spiritually speaking there is an "exercise" we all need to practice that is probably far more difficult than power-lifting for most of us. It's the opposite of picking up and carrying "weight" or "responsibility." It is the opposite of holding onto something that has become burdensome. It is hard when the thing you need to set down is something you have been relying on emotionally. Nonetheless, it must be done.

The "exercise" is *letting go*.

Practice these exercises for at least thirty minutes a day, three times a week, and I guarantee you'll see healthy results in time!

Today,

- Let go of regrets.
- Let go of offenses, old and new.
- Let go of "scorekeeping" in your relationships.
- Let go of someone who needs a healthy change, a move, and new horizons . . . though it will create distance between you.
- Let go of those problems you've been rolling around your head all night instead of sleeping!

It's interesting, isn't it, that you need more spiritual muscle to "let go" than to carry!

nor anybody else knew which patients were prayed for and which were part of the control group. All patients admitted to the coronary care unit in a large county hospital in San Francisco were included in the study, except those who refused to participate or those who were unable to give informed consent. Then 192 patients were chosen by lot to be in the prayed-for group, while 201 patients were not assigned to receive intercessory prayer by the selected intercessors.

The amazing result demonstrated that prayer alone—not suggestion or other psychological effects—had a clear positive influence on the healing of disease. Patients who received intercessory prayer on their behalf, even though they did not know they were being prayed for, did better than those in the control group. They had fewer complications and fewer life-threatening events than those who were not assigned to the group receiving prayer. For instance, the intercessory prayer group had fewer patients

---

The amazing result demonstrated that prayer alone—not suggestion or other psychological effects—had a clear positive influence on the healing of disease.

---

with congestive heart failure, used less diuretic medication, had fewer cardiopulmonary arrests, less pneumonia, and used fewer antibiotics. They were also discharged from the hospital sooner than the control group.[4] No flashy, miraculous, instantaneous results here—just steady improvement, and all-around superior results for the group receiving prayer.

My emphasis on the fact that this experiment was un-contaminated with possible effects from suggestion, the laying-on of hands, the cheering presence of a praying, loving person in the room, and so forth may be misunderstood. I am not saying that these other factors, including the patient's own strong positive belief that he or she is being helped, are not useful. Those additional factors are valuable in actual practice. But by making intercessory prayer *alone* the variable studied, Dr. Byrd was able to show that results were due solely to the power of prayer. I don't know of another experiment that showed so convincingly that intercessory prayer has effects independent of your own mental attitudes and positive expectations.

"I prayed and God healed me." Although people have experienced healing without prayer, even without asking for it,[5] there can be no doubt that prayer heals. The Bible is full of testimonies to the effectiveness of prayer. One of those passages that speaks directly to the issue of prayer for healing could serve as a title for this chapter. "The earnest prayer of a righteous man has great power and wonderful results."[6] As we have seen, it does indeed!

Make the Effort to Pray and Believe

Is it possible that some people do not know how to pray? Of course. Will their efforts count anyway? Of course. Never think the "formal" elements in prayer are what make the difference. It is the heartfelt cry of a believing child to his Father, according to Jesus' teaching about prayer: "When you pray, say, 'Our Father . . .' "

Make the effort to pray. Tell yourself the truths about God, and illness, as you pray. But some attitudes are *not* prayers—wishing, for instance. You may have heard that wishing will make it so, but it won't. If you want healing for yourself or others, ask for it. Yes, God knows what you need, but he says, "Ask!" And then take the time to be silent and listen. Listen as the contents of your heart reveal themselves. If there is doubt, anger, fear, let God replace it with restful trust in him, forgiveness, and hope. Listen for the sure Word he will direct you to, and then believe it.

Nothing Can Substitute Prayer

What about that old question that comes up whenever prayer is discussed by the faithful: "Does prayer change God's mind?" I don't think it's wise to speculate. We do have instances in the Bible where the plain text speaks as though he has changed his mind.[7] Still, we wonder how it can be that a Being who knows all things, including all that is going to happen, could change his mind. I don't know the answer to this question. But I do know we must pray, and nothing we can do or anyone else can do for us will substitute for prayer because nothing can do for us what prayer does.

What is this great thing? In the case of illness, prayer invites God to come into your life, your spirit, your mind, your body, your immune system, your endocrine system, your cardiovascular system, and all the rest of you. It invites him to do what he wants to do. What if his desire is not the same as your desire? Then the best part of your mind, the part that loves and lives the truth, wants to change *your desires* and keep *his*. Because there is no way a reasonable person filled with the Holy Spirit would insist on his or her own will instead of the will of God, who is perfect love. But his will and yours may not clash often because, like you, God wants your good. On those occasions when there is a clash it must be because he understands better than you do what is good for you. At those times, you will want what he wants for you even if it means some initial unpleasantness or pain.

Is Healing *Always* the Will of God?

Some Christians teach that healing is *always* God's will and therefore it *always* happens if the person praying has "enough faith." They think if there is no healing it is because faith was not sufficient. I don't agree that God *always* wills the healing of our bodies here on earth. I like the way Francis MacNutt puts it:

> *Healing is ordinary and normative, but does not always take place.* It is this author's belief that the ordinary will of God is that man should be whole. Usually, a man glorifies God more mightily in every way when he is healthy than when he is sick. Therefore, man can and should pray to God with confidence for healing.
>
> Yet, there are exceptions; sometimes sickness is directed toward a higher good, for the kingdom of God. . . . Consequently, healing does not always take place, even where there is faith.[8]

So the centerpiece of every prayer consists in a spiritual change, bringing the will of the praying person into harmony with the will of the listening, loving, all-wise Father. Nothing else can do this in quite the same way as believing prayer.

Prayer Changes Things—Even If We Don't Know How

I don't profess to understand how it can be, but prayer does change things. There are healings available that are never received because nobody prays. It's as if the gift is wrapped, postage prepaid, and waiting at the "post office"—but the addressee does not call for it.[9]

Some people who have had an enormous amount of

experience with healing prayer suggest that a request for healing be as specific as possible, including physiological changes in the immune system, the cardiovascular system, or whatever is needed. And some also recommend that you try to picture these physiological changes actually happening as you pray—see them with your mind's eye. I see no harm in such advice, unless you make the mistake of believing that your own "mental powers" will heal you. We are never to exalt so-called mind sciences over the power of our sovereign and holy God. We are never to imagine we can use his power to do what we want.

But some of the work involved in creating healthful mental pictures seems to fit in with the value of positive thoughts. These activities may very well strengthen the effect of the mind on the immune system and on other systems—an effect we have seen to be real and useful.

Nowhere does Scripture teach that such exercises are essential for true prayer, nor that they increase the efficacy of prayer. About prayer, we are taught only to "ask." It's so simple. And there is no advantage in adding to the teaching of Jesus in order to make prayer complicated and difficult. Just ask your Father to heal you. And don't give up or stop asking.[10]

Mrs. Erskine's Surgery

Sometimes God's healings are nothing short of spectacular. Kathryn Kuhlman told of receiving a prayer request for a Mrs. Erskine—"dying of cancer in the Tarentum Hospital"—which she read over the air, only to be heard by the stunned patient whose doctors had kept from her the news that she had cancer of the liver from which she could not possibly recover. "Her liver is like your grandmother's old lace curtain," the doctor had told her family.

Mrs. Erskine now prepared to die.

The next day Miss Kuhlman said over the air, "I feel compelled to pray again for the woman at Tarentum Hospital dying of cancer of the liver." She did pray, and Mrs. Erskine shook and cried so violently the nurses began giving her hypodermics. But now something happened—something seemingly impossible.

The patient began to eat ravenously, to gain weight, and to show all the signs of good health. Surgery was now possible, but when the surgeon opened her up he found no signs of cancer—only scar tissue and a healthy liver.[11]

I like this story because it reveals the effects of the patient's thoughts and beliefs as well as the power of prayer. But in the final analysis, all healing is God's work.

Prayer *and* Truth

Because the mind is often overlooked as a source of health, I want to concentrate on the effectiveness of positive thoughts and truthful, upbeat attitudes, yet I don't want to leave the impression that there is only one element in healing. We have an amazing tendency to want to find one secret key when in fact many keys are needed together.

One key is surely God's healing activity in response to prayer. But some people think there is a contradiction in praying *and* seeking medical help. "Don't take medicine or consult physicians or counselors," these people urge, "because then you aren't allowing God to heal you." And I am sure some will say precisely the same thing about making efforts to optimize the functioning of your physical systems by reshaping your beliefs and your thoughts according to the truth.

Healing, whether it is accomplished by prayer, medicine, surgery, vitamins, exercise, or telling yourself the truth is God's work. It is no more God's work when a miracle like the healing of Mrs. Erskine occurs than when a person's blocked arteries are cleared through angioplasty. God alone empowers the healing and the healer, whether the healer is a church elder, a physician, a surgeon, a psychologist, or a patient simply asking God to heal him or to help him renew his thoughts.

In fact, most often, a sick person benefits from a combination of routes by which God's healing grace and mercy can come to bring improvement. Be thankful for all God's good gifts.

Healing, whether it is accomplished by prayer, medicine, surgery, vitamins, exercise, or telling yourself the truth is God's work.

Notes

1. Jeremiah 30:17.
2. You can read the entire fascinating story of this man's healing through adherence to the truth as God spoke it to him in his book *Fighting Cancer With Christ* (Carol Stream, Ill.: Creation House). The book can be ordered from Mjorud Evangelistic Association, 3604 Coolidge N.E., Minneapolis, MN, 55418.
3. H. Richard Casdorph, M.D., Ph.D., *The Miracles* (Plainfield, N.J.: Logos International, 1976). Ten cases of healing following prayer through the ministry of the late Kathryn Kuhlman are presented. Dr. Casdorph submitted all his findings for confirmation of his opinions to an impartial panel of physicians, qualified in various areas of expertise, appropriate to the illnesses discussed.
4. R. B. Byrd, "Positive therapeutic effects of intercessory

prayer in a coronary care unit population," *Southern Medical Journal* (1988): 81: 826–829.

5. Acts 3:1–8, for example. The lame man repeated his routine request for alms, and did not appear to think to ask for healing. But healing is what he got anyway.

6. James 5:16, TLB.

7. For example, Genesis 6:6–7, Amos 7:6, Zechariah 8:14–15.

8. Father Francis MacNutt, *Healing*, o.p. (New York: Bantam Books, 1974). pp. 102–103.

9. James 4:2: "You want something but don't get it. You kill and covet, but you cannot have what you want. You quarrel and fight. You do not have, because you do not ask."

10. Luke 18:1–8.

11. Kathryn Kuhlman, *I Believe in Miracles* (Englewood Cliffs, N.J.: Prentice-Hall, Inc., 1962), pp. 66–76.

Chapter 11

"Immunizing" Your Inner Man

When people who are on the verge of giving up discover a new hope, it's amazing. I have often observed what happens when people learn that while some *circumstances* are beyond their control, their *perceptions* and *meanings* are not. It's the start of a new ball game. Almost overnight I'll hear them say, "I'm feeling better!" Once they experience the power of a changed mind, they go on to enjoy new positive feelings, increased physical strength, and more robust health.

Changing Your Mind

The *New Testament* word for *repent* means, literally, *change your mind.* The Bible's message about the importance of a renewed mind has too often been overlooked. In Mark's Gospel, Jesus told his hearers, "Repent, and believe in the gospel." To put it in other words, "The old mind, set on sin, unbelief, and wrong beliefs does not have to stay that way. You can believe the good news. It consists of truths that will change and renew your spirit, soul, and body."[1] Remember the effect on his body described by the writer of Psalm 32 before he cleared his mind through repentance, admitting and acknowledging his sins? "When I kept silent, my bones wasted away through my groaning all day long. For day and night your hand was heavy upon me; my strength was sapped as in the heat of summer" (vss. 3–4).

You and I must regain the clarity of the psalmist's insight. He understood that his aching bones were not the result of a deficiency of analgesic medication, but of a mind that was out of line with God because of sin. Don't misunderstand; I am not saying that all sickness results from a twisted mind or sinful behavior. But I am affirming that those things the psalmist calls our attention to have an effect on your body.

Let's take a look.

Resentment Can Tie Your Body in Knots

I know a man whose mind is clogged with resentment toward a person close to him, though he stubbornly denies it. His body is twisted, his joints swollen, his suffering intense. A while back, he got a break. Something happened to make him acknowledge his anger loudly and openly, with the result that he was temporarily freed from his simmering resentment. As long as he was frank, he enjoyed a release from his painful disease. Unfortunately, he never got around to dealing with his anger by forgiveness and revised thinking. Instead, he went back to denying his anger and hiding his simmering resentment. Immediately, his anguish and swelling returned. Like all of us, he needed to change the content of his mind. That is called repentance.

You *Can* Change Your Thoughts

Can you really change a mind that has formed well-worn grooves? When you read the *New Testament* or hear someone speak about the need for a changed mind, do you believe that change really is possible? Or do you think of it as religious talk about something intangible and metaphysical? Some Christians unfortunately think that they need to build up their psychological defenses. Instead of admitting weakness and sin they learn to strongly deny and repress negative thoughts and feelings—succeeding only in driving the real trouble underground where it becomes even harder to change. No one has told them what repentance really entails. It's far more than a one-day trip "to the altar"—it means daily confronting false and inadequate views of God, which result in wrong thoughts and actions on our part.

The first step in repentance is to let the Holy Spirit illuminate your mind so you can see plainly the sinful fallacies, errors, distortions, exaggerations, and other falsehoods. Look straight at the content of your mind. Don't hide from the garbage. Don't pretend.

You and I need to see why our natural thinking is often false, stupid, sinful, and senseless. Then we need to grasp eternal truths that build up body, soul, and spirit—truths like the goodness and love of God. We need to tell this to ourselves in place of the old misery-promoting misbeliefs that drag us down. Replacing thoughts and attitudes that wear down our spirit can begin to "immunize" our inner man.

Here are the essential parts of a program of mind changing. Remember, you *can* do it or God wouldn't have made repentance the first step in his message to us. We can approach this plan with confidence that God's Spirit will help us.

The Program

Here are the essential elements in the program I recommend:

1. *Believe you can do it.* Tell yourself, "With the help of the Holy Spirit I can change my mind and my negative feelings and thus strengthen my body's resources for moving toward positive health." Identify any doubts about your ability to change and respond to them in this manner: "Yes, it's true that I can't do this by myself. But God has promised to help me believe the truth by the power of the Holy Spirit, and I know he does not lie. He will give me what it takes to repent—change my mind, my feelings, and my body too. Of course he cannot repent for me. I have to do it every day until my new thoughts replace the old ones and become habitual."

2. *Determine to do it.* For most people, changing an accustomed routine is not enjoyable. Any real change involves work. It takes resolve to resist old habits and dangerous and depressing thoughts.

3. *Notice your unwanted feelings and label them.* Some of the most common ugly emotional traps for people with serious illnesses are: *discouragement, bitterness, resentment, fear, anxiety,* and *hopelessness.* Strange as it may sound, we can get so accustomed to negative moods we hardly notice them. We might even miss them if we actually stopped having them. You may believe it is best to ignore negative moods. But the result may be worse than the feelings themselves. Instead of saying, "I shouldn't feel that way, and I'm going to force myself not to think about it," learn to tell yourself, "I'm going to acknowledge my fear and label it for what it is—then I'll have a

chance to do something effective about it."

4. *Believe you can get better.* Is this hard for you? Know that as you work to overcome your negative, harmful, discouraging thoughts, that little seed of belief will grow and fill your whole inner being.

Get That Notebook Going!

If you are ready to get to work, buy a notebook and on the first page briefly summarize the difficulty or difficulties for which you are seeking help. Also list the ailments for which you are working toward healing or improvement, and, if you wish, the emotional, spiritual, mental, and behavioral problems you see and which you intend to overcome with the help of the Holy Spirit.

Your first page might look something like this sample:

"Marianne's" Improvement Record

On September 4, 1995, I went to see Dr. _____ because I had not been feeling as well as usual. He did some tests and told me he thought I might have _____ . This diagnosis was confirmed by my test results. I was shocked and rather numb at first and could not understand why God would allow me to suffer such a setback. I went through my daily activities like a machine. Gradually the reality began to hit me, and I realized I would have to deal with my emotions and work hard at getting better. I decided I would enlist Dr. _____ as a collaborator but that getting well would be my responsibility. I also decided to work at changing my thoughts. I have discovered the importance of positive thoughts, beliefs, and feelings for the full function of my immune system and other health-preserving systems in my body. I will also examine my lifestyle and habits and make whatever changes might contribute to my journey toward healing. I resolve to rely on God for spiritual strength to accomplish the improvement that he wills for me.

On the next page of your notebook, make three columns, the first column narrower than the others.

In the left-hand column, near the top, write the day, date, and time, and the label you have assigned to the negative emotion you are experiencing. Sometimes we have more than one emotion simultaneously—such as both fear and anger when someone seems to threaten us. Other times we are aware of only one feeling. You can record one or more emotion labels.

Sample—Column 1:

Thursday, Jan. 12, 8 P.M.
Anger

In the middle column record as many thoughts as you can that are producing the emotion(s).

Sample—Column 2:

1. I don't see why no one comes to visit me. Don't they know I'm sick and I have feelings too?
2. Nobody cares about me.
3. My friends are thoughtless and unloving.
4. I have always tried to do what I could for other people when they were sick.

Stop and look carefully at these thoughts and the underlying beliefs they reveal. Ask yourself whether they are true. For instance, is it true that nobody *ever* comes to see you or calls or sends a card? Is it a fact that you don't see any reason why you don't have more visitors? Could you have more visitors or possibly telephone conversations if *you* reached out more? Then ask yourself whether the belief is likely to help you reach your goals or to drag you down. Will it help you have peace with God and with your loved ones and friends? And will it help you feel the emotions you want to feel—positive emotions that push your body toward health? If your answer to any of these questions is no, modify or change the thought before you complete column three.

Consider the unwholesome self-talk and beliefs you have recorded in column two and decide how you can replace them with health-giving, constructive thoughts. Record these in column three.

Sample—Column 3:

1. My friends are not all hard, callous, and uncaring. There are legitimate reasons why I don't have as many visitors as I might like.
2. Some may not know that I am sick; others have visited me and may not realize how much I would like to see them again.
3. It's possible that some people think a visit might be too tiring or stressful for me.
4. I could invite some of my friends to call on me.

As you work on your healing by combating pathogenic thoughts, continue using your notebook to develop a work plan. Some sickness-perpetuating thoughts may plague you, such as:

- I can't change my health; I've tried, but I can't. (Discouragement)
- I'm going to get worse, and finally I won't be able to take care of myself. (Fear)
- I know I'm going to suffer excruciating pain. (Fear)

- If my spouse hadn't treated me so badly, I wouldn't be sick now. (Bitterness)
- I should exercise and rest more, but there are too many demands on me at work and at home. (Stressful thoughts)
- My life is a mess and things are out-of-control. (Stressful thoughts)
- God can't possibly care about me. (Depression)
- My future is gloomy and there is no hope for me. (Depression)
- God ought to treat me better. It's unfair that he has singled me out for this illness. (Resentment)
- I won't recover and I'll probably be dead in a couple of years. (Discouragement and Fear)

Healthy Beliefs and Thoughts

The following thoughts are incompatible with those in the previous paragraph. Use your notebook to list the new thoughts with which you will replace your negative beliefs.

- "I can do all things through Christ which strengtheneth me" (Philippians 4:13, KJV). (Courage to work at change, optimism)
- I have no way of knowing whether or not I will die from this illness, but I know Jesus. Therefore I can live every day to the fullest until he takes me home. (Serenity and fortitude)
- Whenever I die, I know I am still in God's loving care and that Jesus has prepared a place for me with the Father. (The peace of Christ)
- I resolve to love and serve others even while I am ill because that is what gives life meaning for me. (Love)
- I am determined to trust God completely. (Confidence)

- I know God can heal me and I can help myself get well. (Positive aspirations)

"But I Have a Weak Heart. . . ."

Our fear-producing thoughts can be connected with the nature of our illness. Negative expectations can come to us through the media, reflecting inaccurate and unhealthy notions widely held in our culture.

For example, some people who have had a heart attack tell themselves life is over and make themselves depressed and discouraged. Often people with heart trouble think they must not do much of anything, even if their doctors tell them to put a little stress on their hearts with exercise.

Replace the notion that you are a helpless victim with the truth that you can direct many things about your health. View your illness as a challenge to change your level of faith, trust, commitment, and participation in your healing.

"My heart is delicate and stressful," you may say. "I must never allow myself to feel any tension, anxiety, or excitement. Even making love is dangerous for me. I should never be far from help, so camping, hiking, or travel are out of the question. It's important for me to think about my problems; it would be dangerous to stop worrying and forget about my vulnerability."

While you should be wise in planning healthy activities, you need to discard those depressing, anxiety-generating preoccupations and fill your mind with optimism instead. The truth is that eighty percent of heart-attack survivors make a full recovery. You can be one of them if you work at it. Exercise that places stress on your heart and blood vessels at the proper level of exertion is one of the best things you can do for your heart. Replace the notion that you are a helpless victim with the truth that you are a player, that you can direct many things about your health. View your illness as a challenge to change your level of faith, trust, commitment, and participation in your healing. Take responsibility, discuss your healing *with* your doctor rather than assume the responsibility for your recovery is his. Discuss appropriate levels of exercise and other activity.

You Can Reach a Higher Level of Health Than You Have Known Before

Following are some health-building beliefs with which to replace fear-producing thoughts:

- I am now placing my entire body, including my heart and blood vessels, into the hands of God who created them. I resolve to trust him and his will for me completely. I am capable of recovering the level of health I had before I got sick—and I may even become healthier than before. I will talk with my doctor about the right exercise and other activities at each stage of my recovery.
- I will remember that under God I can influence my treatment and that I am responsible for my part of it. This will make a vital difference. I will remind myself that life's difficulties are not necessarily harmful for me. They are challenges that can build trust. I will trust God and release all events and all outcomes to him.

"If I Have Cancer, I Might as Well Give Up!"

Cancer patients, likewise, need to train themselves to have a bright outlook instead of victimizing themselves with mental distortions about their disease. Realizing this, a cancer specialist named Carl Simonton had an inspiration. The thought occurred to him that *the patient might have something to do with the treatment of his cancer.* Dr. Simonton has since shown that people who change their doom-laden thoughts about cancer improve while those who hold on to pervasive pessimism and false beliefs about their situation become worse. According to Simonton, general cultural beliefs about cancer are very unhealthy.[2] Some of them are: "Cancer is a strong disease that devours us from the inside out." "Cancer treatments are miserable, harsh, and painful, and nobody knows if they really do any good." "Having cancer means having a death sentence." None of these commonly accepted notions is correct. But when they are firmly embedded in the mind, they can further damage a person who is already struggling with illness.

Working with patients' minds as well as their bodies, Simonton has formulated three powerful beliefs:

1. The body has a natural ability to heal itself and to overcome cancer. When cancer cells and normal cells are put together in a laboratory, cancer cells have never been demonstrated to attack and destroy normal cells. *Never!* However, under the same conditions, white blood cells routinely attack and destroy cancer cells. Cancer itself is composed of weak, confused, deformed cells.
2. Medical treatment can help your body to heal itself, making it your ally in getting well.
3. Cancer is feedback that indicates a need for change—perhaps that you need to do more of the

things that bring you joy and fulfillment, and
fewer of the things that result in emotional pain;
also that you need to learn to respond to the
stresses of life in healthy ways.

This is a message of hope! Acting on it can help you
to align yourself with your true nature and significantly
influence your body's ability to eliminate the cancer.

Following are some wrong thoughts you may have encountered, coupled with thoughts that can help you
change the negatives.

- *Cancer kills its victims.* Cancer sometimes proves
  fatal, but not always. If you are a Christian, nothing
  will end your life until the hour set by the Lord.
- *There is nothing a person can do to get better.* You can
  help yourself get better by tending to needed spiritual
  change, by replacing fear with fact and truthful interpretations, and by changing some life habits.
- *This cancer runs my life.* I am not a helpless victim. I
  am in control. This disease does not control me.
  "With your help I can advance against a troop; with
  my God I can scale a wall."[3] And I can deal effectively
  with this illness.
- *My situation is hopeless because I have this disease.* Situations are inevitable, but hope is a matter of choice
  and I can and do choose to be hopeful.

While some disordered thinking is specific to certain
illnesses, most harmful beliefs and the need to change
them are found in patients with any serious illness. Severe
arthritis, hypertension, AIDS, tuberculosis, multiple scle-
rosis, lupus, intestinal diseases, and many other such illnesses can create a mental and spiritual battleground on
which our spirit is attacked, using our physical vulnerability as an opening.

You may find your notebook filling up with material such as the following:

Negative Thoughts

- What has happened to me is awful. It shows how cruel life is.
- I cannot forgive. What he did to me is just too terrible.
- How can I have a peaceful spirit and a joyful heart when I have this illness?
- I don't have what it takes to be joyful.
- My whole life is slipping away, sliding downhill.
- I can't expect myself to love unless she changes the way she treats me.
- I don't see what I can do for anybody else when I am so bad off myself.
- I can't control what happens to me. I'm helpless.

Positive Thoughts

- My life is not cruel. It is a school in which I am taught by God, a loving teacher. Some learning is painful but valuable.
- My job is to forgive _____ . I am changing my thoughts about him. Even if what he did was wrong, I am choosing to follow my Lord's example: "Father forgive them," and I forgive him too.
- A peaceful spirit and a joyful heart are not produced by circumstances, but by filling my mind with thoughts and interpretations that produce peace and joy—like all the verses in Psalm 18, for example.
- Joy does not consist in what I have, but in the way I regard what God gives me.
- My whole life is in God's hands, moving in the direc-

tion of healing and fulfillment.

- I resolve to love others, not based on how they love me but because God loves me in spite of the way I have treated him.
- I can give others the most wonderful gift they have ever received by demonstrating that peace and joy can flood a person's life no matter what their physical condition or circumstances are.
- I can *influence* my life, my circumstances, and my illness for better or worse. It's up to me to decide.
- I have discovered how to have hope and I can share hope with others.

A Caution About Illicit "Positive Thinking"

You may be trying to think more positively by now. "Yes," you may respond as you read the foregoing, "I am trying to think positively. But I can't seem to get rid of all my negative thoughts. What can I do?" This raises the question as to whether one should simply deny all negative thoughts so that only positive ideas remain. Some readers have assumed that my books on truthful self-talk are really about *positive thinking*, a term embedded in our culture.[4]

No, I am not talking about *positive thinking*. I am talking about confronting mental lies and wrong beliefs with the truth. By that I mean specifically the truth about God and the way he has created our bodies with the capability of returning to health. Truth is revealed to us in the Bible. The Bible does not teach us to adopt superficially positive speech, nor does it teach us to deny reality. This is not true Christian faith.

If you have a fever of 103 degrees, it is not an act of faith to insist that you are completely well simply because you have prayed. Following are more examples of such "illicit positive thinking":

- "Angry? Me? Over a little thing like that? Of course not!" (Meanwhile, you are steaming because your neighbor has forgotten to return your power saw.)
- "Thanks for your sympathy card, but as a Christian I don't feel bad when someone close to me dies. I know he's with the Lord, and I'm happy." (Meanwhile, you are experiencing painful emotions of grief and even physical symptoms in the middle of the night.)
- "I never have any physical ailments, because I am a Christian and the Bible clearly tells us Christ has borne our infirmities." (Meanwhile, you have used up a fortune in health benefits trying to get some help for your lower-back pain.)

Such denial can produce actual physical symptoms. For when the mind is prevented from expressing distress, it turns in desperation to the body: rashes, headaches, backaches, stomach and intestinal problems, cardiovascular difficulties, and immune-system malfunctioning may occur as the only avenue by which denied emotions can make themselves known.

If you think it is your Christian duty to be so positive that you deny the truth, consider this: *If you must choose between a positive thought and a true thought, always choose what is true.*[5]

Sometimes truth has a negative effect—angering us, causing grief, frightening us. But the *whole truth* transforms those negatives into positives, because God turns evil into good. When you tell yourself the whole truth you don't deny pain or illness, you *defeat* it.

You can face the negative side of truth and arrive at a positive attitude:

- Yes, I have rheumatoid arthritis and it can make my joints swollen and painful. (Negative truth.) But my doctor says this scenario doesn't have to happen and that we can find treatments that will help me to improve and remain active. (Positive culmination.)

- Some of my thoughts are untruthful, even sinful, self-centered, and downright hateful. (Negative truth.) But I have a Savior from sin who has canceled my guilt, nailing it to his cross, so that I am free. Nothing says that I *have* to tell myself sinful and untruthful things. I can refuse to have these thoughts and commit the keeping of my mind to him. (Positive culmination.)

- Some people do die from the illness I have. (Negative truth.) But many survive and get well. There is no reason for me to plan on dying from it. Whatever happens, I will keep a cheerful spirit and love those around me. I will keep reminding myself that my Lord has abolished death, so even if I don't improve physically, I will live forever with Christ. (Positive culmination.)

"For nine of my twenty-nine years, I have been battling melanoma (a malignant skin cancer)," said Lindy Goings of Hercules, California. Lindy's cancer had metastasized and surgery had left many physical scars. But the deepest scars were the mental and emotional wounds caused by fear, bitterness, and resentment. Where was God? Then she became a believing Christian and trusted God through Jesus Christ. She learned of his love and faithfulness, and began to tell herself that he would not allow her to be tempted beyond what she was able to endure.[6] Many surgeries later, a CT scan showed tumors in her abdomen. If the cancer had invaded her pancreas it would be inoperable. But surgeons found no cancer in her pancreas or anywhere else for that matter! Again, in October, the drama was repeated—the scan revealed the presence of abdominal tumors but when surgeons opened her abdomen the cancer had vanished.

The Lord was faithful and Lindy remains cancer-free to this day.

What about this young mother's self-talk? What did she tell herself about her illness? For one thing, she did not gain positive thoughts by practicing denial and repression. She never relied on pretending that she didn't have cancer. To paraphrase what Lindy revealed about her thoughts, they went something like this:

> This is too much for me to bear already and now I must endure another surgery. It's as if God is not listening to my prayers, as if he doesn't understand the hurt and the anger I feel. But no matter how I feel I know that he does understand, and he is faithful. I am his and my life is in his hands. Whatever happens, his lovingkindness continues to shine on me.

Notice that these thoughts are not unadulterated, simplistically positive statements. There are negative elements in them as there are negative elements in reality, in life. *But the culmination is positive as it must always be where God has revealed the truth about his love for us in Christ Jesus.*

You can use this as a model for your own efforts as you go about changing your beliefs and thoughts.

Above all, remember that God himself wants you to enter into the process of repentance. He will help you to face the truth about thoughts and feelings that are keeping you in bondage to an old way of life.

As you begin to try this program for inner renewal, I know you will find remarkable changes occurring. Trust them. And follow on to health and hope.

Notes

1. Mark 1:14–15, RSV: "Now after John was arrested, Jesus came into Galilee, preaching the gospel of God, and say-

ing, 'The time is fulfilled, and the kingdom of God is at hand; repent, and believe in the gospel.' "

2. O. Carl Simonton, M.D., and Reid M. Henson, with Brenda Hampton, *The Healing Journey* (New York: Bantam Books, 1992).

3. Psalm 18:29. This entire Psalm is full of truthful and health-giving self-talk with the power to give you victory over negative thoughts and help you to create positive feelings. Read it daily until it fills your mind automatically.

4. Norman Vincent Peale's *The Power of Positive Thinking* (New York: Prentice-Hall, Inc., 1952) is one of the most popular books ever published.

5. Although recent research into the connection between Christian faith and physical or mental health has produced an abundance of scientific evidence suggesting that the practice of Christianity causes better emotional and bodily health and well-being, a minority of such studies have found no relationship or even an inverse relationship between the two. One cause of this strange finding may be the unfortunate teaching among some groups that Christian faith requires denial of unwanted reality.

6. 1 Corinthians 10:13. Lindy says of this passage: "I have come to rely on this promise and he has kept it faithfully."

Chapter 12

Fine-Tuning Your Life

Lifestyle changes are also very important in forming a climate of inner health. What are the characteristics of a healthy lifestyle?

You may be a person who remains constantly on the go and allows no time in your daily life for prayer. You can say, "Prayer is good. God answers prayer," but a lifestyle that is too busy to pray speaks the truth louder than words. You don't *really* believe that learning to commune with God is good or you would value it more than you value your hectic schedule of activities.

Maybe you value time alone, away from people. When you become depressed you may tend to think, "I have no friends. No one likes me," when in fact you have built an isolating lifestyle. You can *say* you believe friendships are supportive but you need to actively *build* friendships by an investment of time.

Let's take a look at lifestyle changes that you may need to make to reinforce and act on your inner renewal. In

each case I will include an "involvement list," helping you
to devise a practical response and plan. You may want to
include an involvement list in your personal notebook.
Later, you can look back at your reactions when you are
planning your overall program.

There are some lifestyle changes you may need to
make in order to fine-tune your life.

A Take-Things-in-Stride Attitude

Some of us are perfectionists. We think, "If I don't get
everything done, and done well, my life will be miserable."
You try to get everything done at once.

Take it easy! If you are the kind who carries loads of
frustration, learn to simplify. Even when it comes to this
program for change, work patiently and steadily on
change, stick at it, and accomplish real improvement. One
bit of genuine progress is worth more than a roster of
aborted starts.

☐ I take things in stride pretty well now. No need to
change.

☐ I am going to do my program at a measured pace,
one step at a time.

☐ Taking things in stride isn't something I am ready
for yet.

Physical Exercise

Do you feel a twinge of guilt when you drive past
someone who is running for exercise? The evidence in
favor of exercise is strong. Aerobic activity contributes to
health.

I'll spare you the details because whole books about
exercise are readily available. But increasing your heart

and respiration rate for at least thirty minutes three times a week, even by vigorous walking, will do good things for your body, mind, and emotions.

If you are presently a stubborn member of the sedentary class, start your regimen slowly and work gradually up to speed. If you are subject to physical limitations due to illness, consult your physician. And if you are interested in training for a marathon, get expert help. If you change your sedentary habits only enough to get up and help with housecleaning or follow a lawn mower around the yard and do a little gardening, the change will be in the right direction.

If you are temporarily immobilized and unable to exercise at all, you can still do some mental practice every day. Play an imaginary game of tennis or golf, focusing on improving your serve, your putt, or your drive. If you run mentally through a park, you will benefit. You may never notice but when you imagine yourself practicing such skills your body actually takes part and your muscles contract and lengthen as if they were performing the task, only on a subliminal level, which can be detected by sensitive instruments.

☐ I am already exercising as often as I can or should.
☐ I plan to add regular physical exercise (or mental if I cannot now do much physical exercise).
☐ What I plan to do for exercise is to _____ .

Keeping a Pet

Frequent interaction with a pet dog or cat can improve your health. Pets have been shown to have a positive, health-giving effect. Giving love and care to God's creatures can give you back much more than the time and energy you invest.

Turning the Tide Slowly

Habits are best changed over time. Those impulsive decisions to change everything overnight usually wash out to sea pretty quickly. On the other hand, gradual, small changes—practiced faithfully over time—build into healthy ingrained behaviors.

Why not work on the suggestions listed below over a period of time? You will not only feel great about yourself for sticking with it . . . you may want to add a few other changes of your own. A year from now your life could be significantly different.

Exercise:

Add a slow, deliberate stretching exercise to your day. Or a walk. Or climb stairs instead of riding elevators. Stretching out those muscles carefully gets wastes and toxins moving out of your system, ends stiffness, and can give you a wonderful relaxed glow.

Attitude:

Think of a person who you have not forgiven. Begin praying that God will give you an attitude of forgiveness. Don't expect a feeling to come right away. Leave that work of changing your heart in God's hands. You'll be surprised how leaving *yourself* in God's hands will help you to leave the other person and their offense in God's hands too.

Turning the Tide Slowly
(continued)

Service:

Thoughtfulness is the wellspring of true Christian service. If your days are filled with mostly self-serving activities, make a phone call to someone who is lonely or in a tough spot, just to say, "I'm thinking of you." Notice one need that you can easily fill for another person today.

Nutrition:

Keep a record of everything you eat in a given day. (Include everything!) Are you really aware of *what* you eat, *how often* you eat, and *why* you eat? (i.e. because you are bored, lonely, or sad).

If you have been feeling sluggish or bloated, try a half-day or a full-day fast. (Unless you are on medication or otherwise medically unable to do so. Drink juices, if you do fast.) Giving your system a rest from constant food digestion is a good thing to practice—and those rumbles in the stomach won't harm you at all!

☐ I agree, a pet makes a wonderful companion and I
have one or more pets.

☐ I will get a pet—sounds like a fine idea.

☐ If I am able, I will care for my pet's needs myself.

☐ I will not get a pet at this time.

Church Attendance

If you are able to go, attend the services of your
church. I'm not suggesting this merely because I think it
would be a good idea, but because studies show that people who attend worship services regularly are healthier and
live longer than those who don't.

Some Christians have committed their lives to Jesus
Christ and maintain a relationship with him in daily *private* devotion—but they see no value in church attendance. There are many additional spiritual, emotional,
and physical health benefits to be gained from fellowship
with brothers and sisters in Christ. Add church attendance
to your program for increased health and healing.

☐ I attend church services regularly.

☐ I will add regular weekly church attendance to my
program.

☐ I will not add church attendance to my life at this
time.

Laughter

Do you remember the story of Norman Cousins who
treated his dreadful illness with large doses of funny movies? Proverbs 17:22 says, "A cheerful heart is good medicine." Remember that and apply it to yourself.

How long has it been since you indulged in a good
laugh? There is nothing like a hearty laugh for inducing a

good mood or preparing yourself for a good night's sleep.
What makes you laugh? Do you have a special friend with
whom a conversation always guarantees a laugh? If you
do, get together and "laugh yourself well." How about
good comedy movies? Humorous books and collections of
cartoons? Do you enjoy reading joke books? Whatever
makes you laugh, get ahold of it and treat yourself to a half
hour of good humor every day.

☐ I already laugh a lot every day.
☐ I haven't laughed for a long time.
☐ I think I need to laugh more every day. I'm going
    to do it.

Nutrition

An old aphorism states: "You are what you eat." Trite
but true.

Spiritually, mentally, and emotionally we are affected
by what we eat. Evidence shows that certain depressions
can be helped by taking B vitamins, L-tryptophan, and
other amino acids. Some psychiatrists prescribe high
doses of vitamins for certain psychotic illnesses. We know
that low blood levels of cholesterol are related to increased
impulsivity and violence, that potassium insufficiency can
cause depression—and sugar consumption can be related
to anxiety levels.

Few doctors today doubt that the effect of our diet
ranges well beyond its impact on our weight!

There is consensus on the importance of reducing fat
intake, eating plenty of fresh or frozen fruits and vegetables, adequate B vitamins (recently folic acid has been
found to reduce susceptibility to heart attacks and
strokes), and antioxidant supplements, especially *Beta
Carotene, Vitamin C,* and *Vitamin E* (with *selenium*). An-

tioxidants seem to prevent cell damage. Optimal nutrition is a major part of one of the most successful treatment programs for heart attack victims and patients with coronary artery disease. With this program some doctors have succeeded in *reversing* atherosclerosis. Susceptibility to cancer also seems to be related to the amount of fat in the diet.

In the not too distant past most physicians were poorly trained in nutrition. Doctors tended to discount the importance of nutrition for good health. Fortunately, medical schools are now giving more training in nutrition and some physicians have a special interest in the therapeutic benefits of diet. So consult your doctor. Supplements may be in order for you. And so may some specific dietary rules related to your disorder or to interaction with medications you may be taking. Don't look for this brief discussion to give you enough information. Get more fully informed either with an up-to-date book on this vital subject or by consulting a fully trained nutrition expert.

In general, nearly everyone can safely adopt the following practices without fear of going off the deep end:

- Eliminate or reduce your intake of junk foods, including high-fat hamburgers, hot dogs, French fries, potato chips, as well as cream, sour cream, whole milk (substitute skim milk), butter, margarine, fried foods, and other similar agglomerations of fat. (An enormous amount of fat comes hidden in cookies, pie crusts, cake, and cake icings.)
- Cut way down on meats, especially red meats, and dairy products, including cheese, eggs, and butter.
- Increase your intake of vegetables, fruits, and whole grain foods. The current USDA recommended intake is five servings of fresh fruits or vegetables per day. Beans and other legumes, whole wheat, oat, or other

whole grain breads, rolls, and cereals are recommended. Pasta and potatoes are both excellent sources of starch and can be eaten several times weekly.

- Vitamin supplements are safe in moderate doses. A multivitamin/multimineral tablet per day is safe and recommended. In addition, many physicians and pharmacists themselves take supplementary antioxidants daily. These are Beta Carotene (a precursor for Vitamin A), Vitamin C, and Vitamin E.
- Get plenty of fiber by eating whole wheat bread, vegetables, and fruits.

☐ My present diet conforms to most of these suggestions.
☐ I will make some changes in nutrition.
☐ I will study nutrition on my own or ask my doctor for advice.
☐ I am not ready to make any nutritional changes.

Service to Others

Hans Selye, the great stress researcher, called service to others "altruistic egoism." He referred to the trait in some people that causes them to value the goodwill of others, which prompts them to do things to serve other people. The Bible speaks of a similar drive created in believers by the indwelling of the Spirit of God, a desire to help others and serve them *whether thanks are received or not.* The active principle of reaching out and doing things to benefit others has been found to accompany low levels of the stress hormone (norepinephrine) and a better equipped immune system. So when Selye and others advise, "Get some love in your life," they are not talking about making other people give to you. Rather, they extol the benefits of giving to and serving the needs of others.

Churches usually offer opportunities for helping others in many ways. Bringing "meals on wheels" to shut-ins, contributing to or working at the food shelf, calling on the sick, singing for people in nursing homes, bringing Bible teaching to groups in institutions, maintaining church property, mowing lawns, cleaning, and driving for persons who are incapacitated . . . and much more.

But you don't have to restrict your love and service to organized projects. Preparing and bringing food to a bereaved neighbor or a shut-in friend, offering to drive someone to the doctor's office, calling another person who is lonely, offering to pray for another, interceding for others without their knowledge, giving money or goods to meet someone's needs, and offering to help anyone who appears to need assistance are some of the possibilities.

What if you are sick and shut in yourself? Then you especially need to stave off self-centeredness by developing this part of your life. When we suffer from illness or pain it is very easy to become attentive only to ourselves. Nothing could be worse for our spiritual, emotional, *and physical* health than to develop self-pity, resentment, bitterness, or a martyr complex. To get better—to thrive— we must be sure to develop outreach through even simple acts of service and love.

"I can't think of anything *I* can do. I'm so restricted by my own illness," you may say. Ask the Lord to show you those who need your help. I don't know what restrictions there are on your mobility and activity, but perhaps you can write notes of encouragement to others, send cards, draw, paint, or develop crafts to present as gifts, correspond with lonely people on the Internet, develop computer programs, read books into a tape recorder for someone unable to read for herself, or grow potted plants to give away. Most importantly, you can listen to others, dis-

cern their needs, and let the Holy Spirit show you what
you can do.

☐ I resolve now to add to my life more loving service
to others.

☐ I have some ideas. I might be able to _____
_____.

☐ Not right now. I have too much on my schedule as
it is.

☐ I have been doing these things already. I don't see
the need to add more.

Other Additions to Your Quality of Life

Don't forget to play. Whatever you do for enjoyment
counts as play. This includes listening to music, spending
some time outdoors in nature, reading for pleasure, computer games, chess or checkers or other games with someone else, chatting for fun, hobbies, sports (if you can't be
a player, at least you can be a fan).

Did you know that smiling can help? Deliberately wear-
ing a cheerful facial expression can affect your emotions
and reset your autonomic nervous system so it is less re-
active to stress. A happy facial expression can increase
blood flow to your brain and release beneficial neurotrans-
mitting chemicals in the brain. If you are anxious and depressed, making yourself look sunny can actually change
your feelings.

Above all, learn to dialogue with God. He is not far from
every one of us, and he can be especially close in times of
suffering or disability. Dialogue with God is not about formal prayer, but about the habit of companionship with
him in which you listen for that whispered word in the
form (usually) of a thought, and you respond to him or
ask him questions as you would a loved one or respected
companion at your side.

————————

Beyond all these personal approaches to life, it may be time to widen your circle of involvement. Perhaps you feel overrun by personal or family commitments as it is, but the fact is involvement with people outside your home can have many healthful effects.

Consider carefully the lifestyle changes you may need to make, learning to build a healthy web of supportive relationships. We'll look at these next.

Chapter 13

Community

We were created to be part of a community. And so it makes sense that healthy involvement in groups, churches, and organizations will be good for us.

Let's look at your lifestyle as it relates to involvement with others.

Time Spent With Other People

Are you waiting for others to visit you? Are you asking, "Why don't they realize how lonely I am and how much visits mean to me?"

If necessary, make the first move. Reach out. Evidence shows that we all benefit from time spent visiting with others. Even visiting with friends on the telephone can do important things for our health.

Doctors Esterling, Antoni, Margulies, and Schneiderman were aware of a growing body of evidence showing a connection between stressful emotions and immune-system functioning. They were excited by the recent discovery that psychological reactions have a direct effect on diseases related to the immune system. They knew, for instance, that people depressed about a divorce were more likely to be affected by certain viruses than other people. Now they wanted to see if talking about their stresses would actually get rid of viruses already present in the blood. So they arranged an experiment.

Some students who tested positive for Epstein-Barr virus talked or wrote about stressful events. The results were startling. Disclosing their feelings produced a marked decrease in the virus antibodies, demonstrating that immune systems perked up with emotional unloading. Moreover, students who tended to keep their feelings hidden, sometimes even from themselves, turned out to have more of the virus.[1] Talking boosted the students' immune system functioning markedly.

If you are sick with a disease related to immune system functioning (HIV, cancer, herpes, or rheumatoid arthritis, for example), one of the best routes to improvement is in *community*, having other people to talk with. Talking with a counselor, talking with others in a support group, talking with friends—all of these are extremely important.

We are becoming aware of the vital role of the community in creating a healthy life-supporting atmosphere in which we thrive. Community on every level is a gift of God's grace. To a large extent, those around us help determine what we should value and what we should reject. Others model right behavior—and some exemplify wrong behavior and its consequences for us. Our communities encourage or discourage us. When we are in need of support, we turn to our community.

Community and belief go together. Just the other day I noticed how this works with my wife, Candy, and me. When she has trouble maintaining a strong, positive faith in God in respect to some needed blessing, the chances are good that I will be able at such a time to share some of my optimistic God-centered expectations. And when I can't manage much enthusiasm, Candy may very well be overflowing with confident conviction that lifts me with it!

I stress this need for support because too many believers try to go it alone. Consequently, they have a tough time battling their pessimism and natural unbelief. For anyone working on personal change, enlisting the aid of other people only makes sense. This means:

You Need a Church Community in Which You Participate

Not just any church, but one in which the teaching helps you to live differently. If you are looking for a church to help you toward health, you don't need a hatchery of grimness, negativity, or despair. Find one that teaches that we are all sinners but we are not hopelessly and eternally lost if we place our hope and trust in Jesus Christ. Find there God's mercy and love, and the security that nothing is able to defeat you because you are in his will. Look for a fellowship that teaches the truth of the Scriptures and the peace and joy found in Christ. Stay away from the dark, the oppressive, and the doom-dealers. I do not recommend church-hopping, but there are times when the church you are attending can have a negative rather than a positive influence in your life. And there are certainly churches where the truth has long ago been forsaken in favor of moral relativism, feminism, socio-political pursuits—*secularism* under stained glass. There are even churches where Jesus is proclaimed as a great teacher, a stirring speaker, and a good man—but not God. With the loss of truth goes the power for change. If your church has abandoned the truth, leave that church, and find one where the pure Word of God is preached to promote Christian living among its members.

You Need a Doctor Who Will Talk With You

I am assuming you are aiming at acquiring that positive, truthful view of your illness that will enable you to move toward health. That's not going to be easy if you have a doctor who won't listen and can't find time to talk. Your physician should be capable of a special relationship with you in which you feel respected, in charge of your own program, able to share your misgivings with confidence, and get information about symptoms, diagnoses, and your medical concerns. Some physicians may be very good at technical issues but limited in their view of what their work ought to involve.

Occasionally you will find a doctor who thinks of a human being as little more than a complicated machine. In the materialistic philosophy of such medical "experts," a sick human being is merely an *apparatus* with a broken part. If a doctor is going to help, you must be seen as a *person* who happens to have an illness. Great technical knowledge and skills are important but they cannot minister to your mind.

Your physician should be capable of a special relationship with you in which you feel respected.

You will do better to find a competent doctor who understands that your mind and your spirit play a major role in your healing than to continue with a physician who has a one-dimensional conception of his/her patients. Always work with what one writer calls a *healer* as distinguished from a *technician*.

☐ My doctor is a healer with whom I can talk easily and confidently.

☐ I am going to look for a physician who understands the difference between a sick human being and a broken machine, one with whom I can talk with confidence.

☐ My doctor doesn't take time to talk with me and seems interested only in getting my symptoms under control, but I don't want to look for another doctor at this time.

Get Together With Your Pastor Periodically

If you can't go to the church office, the pastor can probably visit you. Discuss your spiritual concerns with your pastor, knowing you will receive insights into God's Word that can help you cope. When I entered the parish ministry, I began making calls on the shut-ins, the sick, and the aged. I discovered something. The shining example of faith exhibited by these saints gave more to me than I, a young, green, inexperienced seminary grad, could begin to offer them—except for the Word and the Sacraments, which I brought to them regularly.

It will be good for you to share your faith with your shepherd. And don't forget to ask for prayer. Don't expect the minister to know automatically what you want. Ask!

☐ I already see my pastor regularly for visits and/or ministry.

☐ I will arrange to get together with my pastor regularly for visits and/or ministry.

☐ This won't be possible for me at this time because

_____

_____ .

☐ I have no pastor at this time.

Join a Support Group

There are all kinds of groups these days. Bible study groups, prayer groups, cell groups, support groups of all kinds can be found in most large cities. If you live in a larger city, you may find a group of people coping with a health condition similar to yours. Ask for help locating people with whom you can meet and share insights. If none exists where you live, start a group yourself.

You can always use extra help by participating with people who are working on problems similar to yours. It may be a Christian group with a spiritual growth aim (like a home fellowship group), or a group of people discussing specific stressful issues such as parenting adolescents or making marriage better.

You need to talk with others about your thoughts and beliefs, especially those that make life events stressful. Flee from groups that spend the meeting time rehearsing misfortunes, recounting misery, and moaning about the unfairness of life. Treasure a group that will join you in pursuit of faith, life, and the best possible outcomes emotionally and physically.

You may not find a support group for your special difficulty, and therefore will have to start one if you really want to seek help among those of like situations. What such a group would do would be determined by the participants. But here are some suggestions:

1. Keep members informed with the latest research related to their illness or difficulty. This could be done by asking experts from the community—for example, doc-

tors, psychiatrists, psychologists, nurses, community health specialists, pastors, religious teachers—to speak to you. Or individuals in the group might take turns researching a subject related to the group's central concerns and presenting to the group what they have discovered.

2. Discuss wise perceptions, spiritually strengthening insights, edifying incidents, signs of progress, courageous steps and decisions, and other encouraging experiences and increased understandings of participants.

3. Work toward solution of problems, resolution of conflicts, correction of erroneous and destructive beliefs of individuals.

4. Celebrate progress and the victories of individuals by getting together for dinners, parties, sports events, picnics, outings, etc.

5. Develop spiritual insight through group Bible studies especially applicable to issues that emerge in the group process. For example, someone might wonder what the Bible has to say about the effect, if any, of praise on depression; or whether the Word encourages us to expect God to heal us; or whether anxiety is a sign of spiritual weakness and depravity.

6. Pray for various persons, situations, and needs. And be a safe confidant where personal secrets are not shared outside the group.

Above all, a group is a *community* for its members. This community must be kept focused on what is encouraging, uplifting, and positive. Everybody should aim at learning the truth and applying it to life situations, resolving conflicts, and developing workable solutions to problems. Obedience to the truth should be stressed so that truth is not merely grasped intellectually but acted out in life. Support for a life of praise and obedience, bringing joy and peace, ought to be the focus of the group's existence.

☐ I already participate in one or more groups.
☐ I plan to find and join a group for _____.
☐ I will start a group for _____.
☐ A group doesn't seem appropriate for me at this time.

See a Counselor or Therapist

You may need to talk with a counselor, a therapist, or a pastor about stressful issues. One Christian radio station features a daily talk-show hosted by a Christian counselor whose stock-in-trade seems to be criticism of other Christian counselors. He insists your counselor must not be a psychologist, nor should he or she use any psychological methods. What fascinates me is that this critical Christian radio host uses psychology himself, and he doesn't know it! In fact, the only substitute for psychology in counseling is poor psychology.

Whether your counselor calls herself a reality therapist, a biblical counselor, or a truth therapist, if you are helped to grasp God's truth by faith—that is, to change your mind and action—that counselor will be of value to you.

But how about those of you who feel negative about seeking help? "I should be able to do it myself," you say. I can understand what you are feeling because that's precisely what I tell my wife while she is urging me to ask somebody for directions: "Honey, I can find it myself!" I know some of you feel personal defeat if you have to ask for help. But wait. I think we're both wrong. There is nothing weak, deficient, inadequate, or stupid about us if we ask for help! Sometimes asking for aid is the intelligent response of a wise person. And likewise, a few sessions with an astute counselor can be a real turning point for you, even if the only illness you have is a physical disorder.

Often a pastor or pastoral counselor will help. A Christian cognitive behavioral therapist would have some useful things to teach you. If you can't find the counseling you need in your community, you can call the Center for Christian Psychological Services.[2] Therapists there might be able to help you in your search or even to work with you on the telephone under certain circumstances.

☐ I have a counselor or a therapist whom I see regularly as needed.

☐ I plan to look for a counselor to help with my program.

☐ I don't feel a need for counseling at this time.

There is nothing weak, deficient, inadequate, or stupid about us if we ask for help! Sometimes asking for aid is the intelligent response of a wise person.

Make Some New Friends

Psychologists have agreed that people who spend time with others, especially those who actively pursue friendships and association with other people, are generally more healthy than those who avoid people. They have found that persons who can love and care about others have lower levels of stress hormones and higher ratios of helper T cells to suppresser T cells, in other words, better immune systems.

☐ I have plenty of friends and an active social and recreational life.

☐ I plan to reach out and make some more friends.

Next, let's take a look at how we can improve our knowledge of God and our relationship with him.

Notes

1. B. A. Esterling and M. H. Antoni, [Dept. of Psychology, Univ. of Miami]; M. A. Fletcher, S. Margulies, and N. Schneiderman (1994). "Emotional disclosure through writing or speaking modulates latent Epstein-Barr virus antibody titers," *Journal of Consulting and Clinical Psychology*, 62, 130–40.
2. The Center can often direct you to a Christian counselor in your area (call 612–633–5290). Center therapists do telephone counseling in some instances. Generally it is best to see you in person first for testing and diagnosis. Then, if you and we decide it is beneficial to proceed we will arrange telephone counseling. These sessions generally require fifty minutes; long distance charges will be billed to your telephone.

Chapter 14

Getting Closer to God

Spiritual activity charges up your immune system, decreases stress, and leads to measurable health benefits. Just as changing your mind about negative behavior makes your entire self better, so immersing yourself in the presence of God will result in spiritual, emotional, and physical improvement.

How do you relate to God? Is it a quick "hello" in the morning? A once-a-week affair at church? Or is your relationship with God strained because you feel he's let you down? Or is it just that you've never given it much attention? Making God part of your whole life means taking a look at some spiritual habits and making needed changes.

Following are some important areas to consider:

Studying the Bible

Daily immersion in God's Word is a therapy you will want to utilize in the most effective way. Will reading the

Bible advance good health? Perhaps it sounds like a novel idea, or wishful thinking, even superstition. But it is true! Several studies have shown a striking correlation between health or longevity and various indicators of religious commitment, including Bible reading and prayer. As a force for deep spiritual commitment, the habit of daily Bible reading can help you have better spiritual, emotional, and physical health.

Don't just read a daily ration of verses like a quota of push-ups. Stop and think. Wonder about it. Ask the Holy Spirit for light.

If we hadn't been hammered by cultural forces with materialistic assumptions, we would think it obvious that health benefits come from nurturing our spirits with the Word because "All scripture is inspired by God and profitable for teaching, for reproof, for correction, and for training in righteousness, that the man of God may be complete, equipped for every good work."[1] Because proper use of the Bible makes believers complete, equipped, and trained in righteousness, and because God's Word corrects our erroneous beliefs and habits of spirit and mind, we would do well to work on developing a voracious appetite for Bible reading.

Schedule at least fifteen minutes daily for Bible study. Rather than flit around, read a single book chapter or so at a time until you have read and digested that book. Don't just read a daily ration of verses like a quota of push-ups. Stop and think. Wonder about it. Ask the Holy Spirit for light. Pose questions as you read, and try to find answers. Let answers suggest more questions. Pay special attention to items in the text that combat your negative, false, misleading beliefs and let those items work healing on your mind.

As you read, ask yourself, "What does this sentence say to my beliefs, my thoughts, my misbeliefs?" You may notice, for instance, that a certain Bible text says, "You are not under the law." But wait! If you stop to examine your own thoughts, you may realize you often put yourself under "laws"—telling yourself you must obey certain rigid rules like:

"Cleanliness is next to godliness."
"Always be right on time or you're a bad person."
"Never give up on anything you start."

Some people bug themselves with man-made rules as if they were the essence of faith. They torment themselves with fabricated "laws" until their lives are miserable. Let your own thoughts out for air, and take a look. If you are "not under the law" it might mean you can begin relaxing some of your self-imposed rules. Let this sweet truth dawn on you: Your life doesn't flow from a book of dead rules, but from the living Spirit of Jesus Christ within you.

Suppose, for instance, the text you are working on happens to be in Romans 8. Here is one way to "get into a conversation" with the Word. In the first column below I have copied some verses from Romans 8 of the Revised Standard Version of the Bible. In the second column I have written some sample notes like the ones you might make in your notebook. Remember, your notes have a specific purpose: to lead to changes in your beliefs and thoughts.

A Sample of Bible Study Notes

Romans 8:1—There is therefore now no condemnation for those who are in Christ Jesus.

No condemnation? I certainly feel condemned sometimes, and I know I don't always do right. But God says here I am not condemned for my sins because I am "in Christ Jesus." But I wonder. Am I really "in Christ Jesus"? Yes, I am because I believe in him as my God, my Savior, and my Lord.

8:2—For the law of the Spirit of life in Christ Jesus has set me free from the law of sin and death.
8:3—For God has done what the law, weakened by the flesh, could not do: sending his own Son in the likeness of sinful flesh and for sin, he condemned sin in the flesh,
8:4—in order that the just requirement of the law might be fulfilled in us, who walk not according to the flesh but according to the Spirit.

These verses are not easy to understand in detail, but one point is clear to me: God has taken care of my sins by condemning them in the flesh of Christ so that I am free to walk according to the Spirit. I guess "walk" means "live." I had better make up my mind to live according to the Spirit! I guess this means I need to let him tell me the truth and stop listening to my old death-dealing thoughts.

8:5—For those who live according to the flesh set their minds on the things of the flesh, but those who live according to the Spirit set their minds on the things of the Spirit.

Well, there it is. Just as I was thinking. He's telling me what I should be doing with my mind. Instead of setting it on the flesh and the things of the flesh, I need to set my mind on the Spirit. This sounds like what I've been reading in my healthy-mind book. First, it says I can "set" my mind. I used to think my thoughts just happened and there was nothing I could do about them. But I have had some success with changing them now, and here God's Word has it plain and clear. I don't have to set my mind on my old thoughts. But I will set them on the new ones, the true ones, the thoughts generated by God's own Spirit and Word. This is great. I *can* do it.

8:6—To set the mind on the flesh is death, but to set the mind on the Spirit is life and peace.

I have already experienced this. When I set my mind on negative, lying thoughts it is downright deadly. I can feel the death in my emotions. And when I set my mind on the Spirit's truth and positive beliefs I can feel the life and peace touching every part of me. Oh Lord, I want to be in touch with the Spirit and his life and peace all the time! I choose to set my mind and thoughts on that every time. And every time my thoughts drift into a negative death-dealing mode I'm going to set them on thoughts that bring life and peace.

8:7—For the mind that is set on the flesh is hostile to God; it does not submit to God's law, indeed it cannot; 8:8–9—and those who are in the flesh cannot please God. But you are not in the flesh, you are in the Spirit, if in fact the Spirit of God dwells in you. Any one who does not have the Spirit of Christ does not belong to him.

I know that I belong to Christ because he has said that whoever believes in him belongs to him. I'm taking verse 9 into my mind and thoughts right now: "*I* am not in the flesh, *I* am in the Spirit, because in fact the Spirit of God dwells in *me*."

8:10—But if Christ is in you, although your bodies are dead because of sin, your spirits are alive because of righteousness.
8:11—If the Spirit of him who raised Jesus from the dead dwells in you, he who raised Christ Jesus from the dead will give life to your mortal bodies also through his Spirit which dwells in you.

Yes, my body will die someday, but my truth-filled spirit is alive. And look at this: The Holy Spirit will give life to my mortal body. I am taking this to mean for me that he will, by his truth and quickening power, cause me to progress toward healing and health according to the will and timing of the heavenly Father.

You can use your notebook to jot down your own thoughts and those suggested to you by the Spirit. You can, if you wish, use my notes as a sort of model. Study your own notes often to recall what God has been saying to you and what your reactions have been to his messages.

☐ I am already studying the Bible every day or nearly every day.

☐ I am going to study the Bible more often, but not daily.

☐ I am going to study the Bible daily, and I plan to ask questions and reshape my thinking as suggested above.

Intensive Prayer Practice

We have already seen some concrete evidence that God answers prayer. So I don't intend to dwell on that, although there are times between the prayer and the answer when our faith is severely tested and we need to remember that prayer to the Father through Jesus Christ is always answered in some way.

Another fact about prayer: the mere practice of prayer is beneficial. Apart from the answer itself, the act of *spending time praying* will make an important contribution to health. "Calling on God" (a phrase used in the Psalms for prayer) leads to reduction of fear and tension, increased confidence, and the security of being close to One who is able to do *anything*. One man put it this way:

> I called upon the LORD in distress: the LORD answered me, and set me in a large place. The LORD is on my side; I will not fear: what can man do unto me?[2]

You can tell yourself truthfully that this great Being, God, is close to you when you pray.[3]

Can you see what that truth can do for your inner being? Certainly all this and more results from spending plenty of time in prayer every day. But there is another major reason for practicing prayer—we may not hear about it much because we're always looking for results, benefits, and a personal payoff. But it is a good reason and we ought to pray for this reason alone: *It is good to pray.* It's true that nothing has better promises attached to it than prayer. But prayer itself is an intrinsically good thing to do. That is reason enough to include regular, serious prayer in your program.

☐ I already practice regular, daily, serious prayer.
☐ I will include serious, regular (at least daily) prayer in my change program.

What about the rest of your busy life, though? How do you begin to carry the truth of God *with you* as you go about your day?

I'll show you one simple practice that can spiritually charge you up all through the day.

Notes

1. 2 Timothy 3:16–17, RSV
2. Psalm 118:5–6, KJV
3. Psalm 145:18

Chapter 15

Creating a Restful Spirit

Meditation is a practice that concerns and frightens many Christians. Although New Age gurus and Eastern mystics promote meditation and relaxation techniques to get their followers into altered states, we do not need to confuse true Christian practice—and good spiritual health—with false spirituality. Because gurus and mystics cook their food, should I stop cooking mine? Because they empty their minds to reach vacant "oneness" with the cosmos, should I stop meditating and learning to refocus my whole being on God so I can fill my heart and mind with the knowledge of him?

In reality, what other religions promote as meditation counterfeits a spiritual discipline grounded in Scripture and practice. For centuries true Christians seeking to draw closer to the Lord have meditated on God and his Word. And they have renewed their spiritual stamina and bettered their health. The average believer today has little familiarity with the meditation methods used by Christians

from the past. It may astonish them to learn that devout
Christians long studied meditation as a way of drawing
nearer to God. Wanting "to be knit to God in spirit, in
unity of love, and accordance of will,"[1] these believers
learned to put away the distractions of life in order to think
the thoughts of God. The great St. Augustine resolved to
"pass beyond [ordinary everyday mental processes, mem-
ories, and thoughts] that I may approach unto Thee, O
sweet Light."[2] Martin Luther, too, recommended prayer
in which one concentrates solely upon God, and he in-
structs us to achieve a spiritually forward attitude by con-
centrating mentally on the words of the Lord's Prayer, the
Ten Commandments, the Psalms, and the sayings of Jesus
or Paul.[3]

It is truly regrettable that although a rich tradition of
Christian meditation literature exists from both the Eastern and Western Christian churches, the only meditation
many Christians have heard of is that promulgated by the
Maharishi Mahesh Yogi. Transcendental Meditation—a
yogic technique adapted by the Maharishi and his followers—and other practices from non-Christian religions
achieved widespread popularity in America a few decades
ago. Many evangelical Christians know they ought not
practice Transcendental Meditation but would be hard
pressed to explain why. They may not realize that the
problem is not meditation itself, but the *forms* of this un-
christian exercise. Pagan religious elements, including the
mantra—the secret word transcendental meditators are in-
structed to use—are unscriptural and dangerous. No believer wants to serve an idol, even unwittingly.

So why meditate at all? Because Christian meditation,
drawing near to God inwardly, is spiritually healthy. "[It
is] good for me to draw near to God"; "Draw near to God
and he will draw near to you."[4] It is emotionally and physically healthy as well. People who meditate faithfully on

Take a Walk Through the Bible

You can give yourself a real spiritual boost, *and* come to know God in more intimate ways by remembering his powerful acts on behalf of people whose stories appear in the Bible. Instead of rehearsing your own situation over and over in your mind, spend some time recalling what God has done for others who felt abandoned, in trouble, ill, in need of forgiveness. . . . Whatever your spiritual state, you can find someone on the pages of Scripture who has dealt with the same conditions you are in. God intervened for them, and he will for you. Trust him.

These are some stories to read and meditate on. Imagine yourself in the shoes of:

- Moses with nowhere to go but through the Red Sea while a powerful, hostile force pursues him from behind.
- Joshua facing the "unconquerable" problem of Jericho.
- David, when his renegade son Absalom takes over his father's throne.
- Job (at the end of his story) when crying out to God brings a new "vision" of God's might and goodness, renewed hope, and a new lease on life!
- the apostle Paul singing in prison.
- the apostle Peter on the shores of Galilee, when Jesus forgives him for his terrible sin and betrayal.
- all those angels and saints around the throne in heaven, filling the book of Revelation with cries of "Holy, holy, holy are you, Lord."

God and his Word at least once a day describe their experience as calming, peaceful, and an antidote for stress. Perhaps something like this is the import of the words, "Be still, and know that I am God."[5] God knows that the clamor and noise of life can block out the awareness of his presence. You can't hear the still, small voice when your own thoughts, your daily concerns, compete for attention. As you will see, the simple technique of focused meditation quiets the clamor and allows the nearness of God's Spirit to become a reality. Just as a nap refreshes your body, so quiet meditation can refresh your spirit, your emotions, and even your physical health.

People who meditate faithfully on God and his Word at least once a day describe their experience as calming, peaceful, and an antidote for stress.

Remember that stress *is not* merely something in the environment that bears down on you until the weight becomes too much. It is *your reaction* to events, including your stressful emotional and physical responses. We have abundant evidence that Christian meditation brings release from the tension and revved-up autonomic nervous system responses we find so disagreeable. In fact, combined with the new thoughts filling your changed mind, meditation will reverse the stressful impact of even traumatic events.

In addition to finding in Christian meditation a way to draw nearer to God—to "be still, and know" his presence—you can also enjoy beneficial physical effects. Here are some of the physiological changes occurring during meditation: drop in oxygen consumption; decrease in the rate of metabolism; increase in slow brain waves (alpha waves); a marked decrease in blood lactate (some experts believe lactate is associated with anxiety); decreased sympathetic nervous system activity (opposite of the fight or flight response) so that heart rate and respiration rate decrease. Blood pressure also decreases in people with elevated blood pressures. All these changes counter stress on an emotional and physiological level.

How to Draw Near

As you can see, benefits to the whole person—spirit, soul, and body—can be obtained by the practice of Christian meditation. But how can you learn to quiet your mind and body before the Lord?

First, select the object on which you will focus. Again, this is the chief distinction between non-Christian meditation and meditation we see in Scripture and church history. Your focus may be a petition of the Lord's Prayer, any other biblical verse or phrase, or even the name of Jesus. You may use the "Jesus Prayer": "Lord Jesus Christ, have mercy on me."

Choose a quiet place that lessens your chance of distraction. Prepare to assume a quieted attitude—not that of the high achiever who might approach this prayer as another mountain to be conquered. Disregard distracting thoughts and dismiss all worries about how well you are doing. (If you become distracted, don't be discouraged or upset. Just return your focus to the word or words of your verse or prayer.) Your posture should be comfortable, relaxed, restful, but not sleep-inducing!

Close your eyes, deeply relax all your muscles beginning at the top of your head and moving on down to your feet. Pay attention to your breathing. Inhale deeply—then exhale and focus on your prayer or verse. Breathe easily and naturally, and continue. Keep this up for ten or fifteen minutes or more, as you wish. After you finish, sit quietly and give thanks to the Lord.

You might begin to practice daily, ten minutes in the morning and ten minutes in the evening. Over time, you will notice that the quiet mind and spirit you cultivate will stay with you as part of your life. And there is a great likelihood that your new attitude will positively impact your health. Conservative estimates point to stress as a major contributing cause of 75 percent or more of all illness. Especially for those with *anxiety problems, hypertension, coronary diseases,* and other *disorders related to stress,* the physical and emotional benefits of meditation can bring positive, life-enhancing changes. And there is some evidence that the relaxation skills developed with regular meditation also actually improve the health of the immune system by increasing the number of helper T cells.

The positive effects of a daily bath in the nearness of God and his peace will provide a range of non-specific gains for nearly everyone.

☐ I will include Christian meditation twice a day in my program.
☐ I will meditate at least once a day.
☐ I will not adopt Christian meditation as a part of my program at this time.

The more you dwell on God and his Word the more you will find the Word of God beginning to "season" your soul at deeper levels. You'll find yourself more firmly convinced of the power embedded in the great truths of Scripture. And you'll find a greater attitude of trust in God.

Trust—a deep, abiding sense of inner rest—is one of our most powerful defenses in our stressful lives. But how do we get it—and maintain it—when we're constantly challenged?

That's what we'll discover as we put together all that we've learned so far.

Notes

1. From *The Cloud of Unknowing,* a fourteenth-century book describing for believers methods of drawing nearer to God. Cited in Herbert Benson, M.D., *The Relaxation Response* (New York: William Morrow and Co., 1965), p. 80.
2. A passage from *Confessions* is cited in *The Relaxation Response,* p. 80.
3. Ibid., pp. 81–82.
4. Psalm 73:28, KJV; James 4:8, RSV.
5. Psalm 46:10.

Chapter 16

Surrender to Love

Elena, a high school math teacher, looked at me and said, "I'm confused. At church I've heard that the key to the Christian life is to *let go and let God*. Now you're saying that I can change things myself—rebuild my immune system and minimize the effects of lupus. So, are we supposed to work on these things ourselves or are we supposed to say, 'Have thine own way, Lord'? Which is it?"

I didn't blame Elena for being perplexed. One day we're told to get busy because things don't happen without our efforts, and then we're told that our problem is that we're working too hard and need to get out of the way.

We need both perspectives.

There are times when there is literally nothing we can do about a situation. Then we do well to give up all striving and depend completely on God's sufficiency. Remember: Whether or not our physical circumstances change, *God is love*.

But there are other times when we know that God is

encouraging us to use the power, wisdom, guidance, and strength that he gives us to solve our own difficulties. It's not what we do alone, but what we do with God's help that makes the difference.

And here's my point: there are things we can do in the realm of our thoughts and self-talk, nutrition and exercise, rest and meditation, that can completely turn around negative health situations. In this case, surrendering to his love means actively working against lies and fears that would swallow us up.

To progress toward wellness we are to work at the task. Along with doctors and counselors, we are collaborators with God, using available facts about our bodies and minds to help ourselves, with his blessing and aid.

We have already discussed working to change your mind, your nutrition, your activity level, your social activities. Now in this closing chapter let's look at some powerful defenses against our great enemies—fear, hopelessness, bitterness, resentment, and dread of death. Not that we need to consider ourselves failures if we do not utterly eradicate these things. Our idea of good work is that which makes even the first steps of progress!

Fighting Fear

Fear is a very real enemy, especially if your condition happens to be one that sometimes results in impairment, incapacitation, or death. Fear is an enemy, even to healthy people who are prone to rehearsing all the bad things that *can* happen. Fear comes in many forms. The threat of rejection, being unloved, losing someone dear, failure. Many people fear impending financial shortfalls. Crushing the power of fear will facilitate healing.

You can begin by writing in your notebook some of the

events or conditions you fear. *Face up to them without trying to cover up.* Spell out the fearful thoughts connected with each one.

Below are some of the fearful thoughts clients have described to me:

> "I am going to suffer terrible pain if this disease gets much worse, and I won't be able to tolerate that much pain."
>
> "This treatment is going to make me so miserable I would probably be better off staying sick."
>
> "If the doctor finds something terribly wrong, I know I won't be able to handle it."
>
> "We don't have enough money to meet our expenses. We could lose our home. We could be on the streets. Worse yet, my family could leave me and I would be all alone—helpless and in agony."

Can you get free from fear? The answer is yes. And it's a process, usually not an instantaneous break. Start formulating good positive responses to fear. These are some responses made by others:

> "I may have to suffer a good deal of pain, or I may go through this illness with very little pain. I know there are wonderful new medical techniques for dealing with pain, and I also know that I will tolerate whatever comes, because God will enable me at the time to manage what I must deal with."
>
> "I don't know yet how uncomfortable this treatment will make me, but even if it does make me sick for a while, it won't last forever. Getting better is worth some temporary distress."
>
> "Even if the doctor finds some problem, my body has enormous power and sophisticated mechanisms designed by the Creator to heal itself. I will likely get

better—in fact, the sooner most problems are treated, the better."

"I cannot know whether we will lose our home or not. And the same goes for all my other negative predictions. I cannot know ahead of time how well I'll cope with unwelcome changes. But I can know that God will give me whatever I need to get through whatever may happen."

Prayer against fear: My Father, I know fear comes from running away and refusing to face reality. When I let fear take over, instead of combating it, I keep myself in a state of tension and heartache. I know freedom is close at hand for me because your Word says that perfect love casts out fear, and I trust in your perfect love. Renouncing fear now, I rest in you at this moment. You are the Rock that cannot be shaken. Nothing can hurt me because I am rooted and grounded in Christ Jesus, my Savior and Lord. Amen.

Facing your fears: Choose a time when you can be quiet and a place where you can be alone. Take a comfortable seat or lie down on your back. Relax or spend a few minutes focused on God and his Word until you feel calm, quiet, and in the presence of the God of Love and Goodness. Remaining calm and relaxed, picture yourself in the situation you have been avoiding, even envisioning the various possible scenarios, from the "better than you expected" to the "worst you can imagine." Replace your fearful thoughts with new, fear-diminishing thoughts. Say those new thoughts to yourself, preferably aloud. Stay quiet and calm throughout this exercise. If you should become tense or anxious, stop your thoughts and relax or meditate until you are calm, then resume. With practice your ability to picture feared situations and to come up with changed thoughts while remaining relaxed will improve. Do this exercise twice a day or more until your fears leave or diminish markedly. Methods similar to this have been proven effective in my clinical practice as well as in numerous experiments.

Developing Hopefulness

Increased pain and weakness, your own preconceptions about illness, worried looks on the faces of doctors or relatives, or someone's doom-laden predictions may all be open doors through which hopeless thoughts enter. Hopelessness brings a heartsick mood and worsens your condition. Instead of giving in, begin to battle hopelessness. *This is vital.*

Prayer of hope: Your Holy Spirit has shown me that you raised your Son from the grave. He is my living Lord, so I will not give up hope even in the most difficult conditions. My strong Lord is still alive today, so my hope rests on firm ground. I have heard the liar whispering, but I resolve to stand firm against despairing thoughts, for they lead nowhere except to sadness and more sickness. Thank you for giving me solid reasons to expect the best. Like Abraham who against the probabilities continued to hope, I will continue to hope regardless of what happens because my hope is anchored in you! Amen.

Internalizing hopeful thoughts: Several times a day try to be quiet and alone for twenty to thirty minutes. Relax and rest. Take a few deep breaths. Practice Christian meditation, remembering you are in the presence of your Rock, your Fortress, your Deliverer, and nothing can hurt you in the ultimate sense. Read the following, preferably aloud, several times each day until these thoughts become automatic—until they replace hopelessness:

> I am determined not to be *afraid* to hope. I resist the devil's suggestion that "hope will be dashed, so it's better not to hope." God's Word says I can and

should hope—and hope that comes from suffering will not leave me disillusioned. Even if things are dark and very hard now, there is nothing wrong with hope. I am still alive and able to pray and change my behavior. I can do the things that lead to health, recovery, or improvement. There are people who improve, survive, and recover even from the most fearsome diagnoses. Even if I feel sorrowful, down, and cheerless, my feelings do *not* mean I have no reason to hope. Because hope is healing, I will keep hoping. If I resolve to hope in him, God will strengthen my heart, and I will soon be praising him for his help. I am at this moment energetically rejecting any thoughts that allege that I will probably die and that it will be awful if I do. This cannot be so, for death has been robbed of its sting in Jesus' resurrection. Eventually, like everyone else, I will pass from this life and be raised to a new eternal life. For now my courage and resolve will lead to God's strengthening.

Exercises: Use your notebook to jot down your own hopeful reflections and possible additions to the above exercise. Make notes on the work you do, or the results of the work you do, as you feel is appropriate.

1. Read about Abraham, who hoped against hope, in Romans 4:13–25. Read it again, putting your name in the text in place of Abraham's. You can do this because, according to Paul, the promise applies to all those who hope in Jesus Christ.

2. The Bible in various places advocates the practice of remembering how God in the past has fulfilled his promises. The effect of this is to strengthen faith. Remember occasions in your own life when your thoughts tempted you to give up hope. Think of times when you seemed unlikely to succeed in school, in career issues, in love, in efforts to make a friend, in winning approval from

someone important to you. If you are currently depressed, it will be even more difficult to remember how God has helped in the past because your memory at this time will tend to be *selective*. It will be much easier to remember discouragements and defeats than to remember successes and victories. If this is your difficulty, it is even more critical for you to do this exercise.

3. Call someone, visit someone, or invite someone to visit you who you know has had a hope-testing experience and emerged victorious. Ask that person to retell the experience to you and how hope persisted in was finally rewarded. This might call for some discernment. Whatever you do, don't invite someone who is going to spread gloom for you. Make clear from the outset that you are trying to build hope and you think they might be able to help you. If they can't, it's better to thank them and tell them you need to look further.

4. Relaxation practice. After you are deeply relaxed and feeling comfortable and tension-free, review the prayer of hope and ponder the hopeful thoughts cited above.

5. Thank and praise God for increasing your resolve to have hope.

Make necessary notes in your notebook. Then take a break from working on your healing and do something restful and relaxing or recreational. Don't do any more work until tomorrow.

Decreasing Bitterness and Resentment

Someone has hurt you terribly. It may have been long ago or recently. Perhaps the harm done was major, perhaps it was not a big deal but still hard for you to get over. Or maybe you repress and deny your hurt and anger. As a result, you have trouble because you did *not* get upset or angry, resentful or bitter over things others have done to you. You have decided this may impair your health or retard your healing as well.

Prayer against bitterness: Solemnly, in your presence, Father, and before the Cross of Christ, I renounce my bitterness and resentment toward _____ . I now receive your love in my heart. It is enabling me to forgive for what was done to me. Whether intentional or unintentional, I was hurt and offended. I stand against those feelings and the thoughts that create and feed my frustration and anger. I determine to do battle against bitter thoughts whenever they slip into my consciousness. With the help of your Holy Spirit, I set _____ free. And I choose to be free from the destructive powers of resentment and bitterness, in Jesus' name. Thank you for the peace and release you give in exchange for my rancor. Amen.

Spite-dissolving thoughts to internalize: Read this to yourself, preferably aloud, several times every day until these thoughts become automatic and the resentful thoughts fade away. Let yourself relax or meditate until you are calm and full of peace before you read.

> I am now going to face the issue of forgiveness. Maybe I have been avoiding it, fearful of my own inability to truly forgive, or concerned lest forgiveness produce more repression and denial. Maybe I am simply unwilling to let my abuser off the hook. Right now, I face the truth: I don't need any special ability to declare to God that I forgive and I don't need to worry if the angry feelings don't dissolve immediately. They may or may not linger for a time.
>
> Repression and denial are a result of *not* forgiving; they are not the same as forgiving—in fact, forgiving is an alternative to these unwholesome tactics. Forgiving does not let the abuser off the hook; it turns the abuser over to God for his dealing, and it lets *me*

off the hook of bitterness, anger, and ill-health!

I am exercising my will to reject every imaginary act of revenge, every wish for another's harm, and every hate-filled image. I believe that God's love is now flowing into my heart (whether I *feel* loving or not) and that it is overthrowing the dominion of hate and anger and the bitterness of unforgiveness.

As God's love grows greater in me at this moment, my negative thoughts toward _____ are fading and melting away and I am rejoicing in the peace that passes all understanding. God's Word promises, "Forgive and you will be forgiven!" Right now while I am forgiving and accepting _____ in love, God continues forgiving and accepting me for Jesus' sake. It feels satisfying to be released from my own guilt and it feels refreshing to get rid of the heavy load of anger and resentment that have been burdening my heart and polluting my being.

Again I declare it before God: I forgive _____ . I release _____ to God. I want the best for _____ .

I am not worrying about how to express this nor about the devil's threat that the bitterness will return later. Right now, for this moment, I am free and I am being made whole—as my immune system, my endocrine system, my hormones, my neuropeptides, my muscles, my heart, my intestines, and my blood vessels respond with their own healing to this release and freedom. My heart beats more easily because it no longer has to force blood through the tightened-up muscles of my resentment. Because my muscles are no longer tense with anger and my chest is not constricted I am going to breathe more deeply right now. (Take several deep, slow breaths, exhaling each one slowly and noticing the relaxation through your spirit, mind, and body.) It feels so good to be free and to let _____ go.

Exercises:

1. In your notebook, on a page titled "Release From Resentment and Bitterness," list the names of those people in your past who have hurt you. Work on a new name each day and then *draw a line through the name.* You may need to work for more than one day on a given name. Remember that when you have sincerely chosen to forgive and worked it out between you and God, it is truly accomplished, whether you feel the results right away or not. *Keep answering the bitter thoughts that may assail you with the truth that you have forgiven and released the person who wronged you.*

Believe it. It is real. When you have finished the entire list, you will want to maintain your freedom by attacking resentful thoughts with truth.

2. Depending on circumstances and the direction of the Holy Spirit, you may want to make plans to write to or call the person or persons you have released or to renew your relationship with them. If this is impossible or for whatever reason you are not ready to do this, note that also.

3. There is evidence that sometimes it is best to tell the person with whom you are angry. Perhaps this is because the purpose for which anger was installed into our emotional repertoire is constructive. It is meant to lead to correction and healing. If this happens to be the case here, and you feel so directed by God to give *positive correction,* you may want to use the following as a guide:

- Tell the other person you want to heal the relationship and to do so it would help you if you could discuss a problem you have had.
- Tell the other person *your own* feelings and perspective. "I have felt hurt by your _____ " rather than "You made me feel so bad and . . ." The pain is

your problem, and so is the anger.

• Ask the other person to change, if this is appropriate, and specify how you would like the other to do things differently. "Would you be willing to _____ from now on?"

Make any notes you wish to make in your notebook, then stop working for the day.   •

Working to Overcome Fear of Dying

Prayer accepting death: I am prepared to recover from this illness and to live a life of joyous love and service for as long a time as I am given on this earth, but I am also prepared to leave this world and be with Jesus. Even if I recover from this sickness I know I will leave this world someday, according to the loving will and plan of my Father. With the power of the Spirit who has already made me dead to sin and alive unto God, I discipline my mind and feelings to gladly go the way God has laid out for me. And whatever that way may be, I know it is for my best good.

Talking to yourself about dying, to release yourself for living. Think through your Christian beliefs about dying. What do you understand dying to be? Do you think of how Christ has transformed death from a stinging wasp to something natural and harmless? For believers, death is the temporary end of physical existence—temporary like sleep, because we will wake up again. Meanwhile we do not cease to exist but simply pass from one phase of life to another. In this new phase we will occupy ourselves with things other than pain, sickness, grief, sin, and death because those things and every other evil will be completely done away with.

Imagine what Jesus has done to disarm death. Great

inner peace is wrapping you in exquisite love—the love of God penetrating every cell, every nerve fiber, every bone and muscle. Gradually, you are moving out of your body, your soul and spirit borne upward by angels. You are marveling at the wonder of it all. You have no fear, no pain, no regrets. Perhaps you say to yourself, "So this is what death is like! This is what we fear and resist for a lifetime and then, when it comes, there is no sting. We are simply swept into the presence of God."

Consider the words of poet John Donne: "Death, be not proud, though some have called thee mighty and dreadful, for thou art not so. . . ."

When you come into the presence of God you will recognize that you have always been closer to him than your own breath. Your body is not needed again until the resurrection. You realize he was always with you, but now you are in his visible presence forever. You have entered into the heartbeat of the universe, the nerve center of everything.

Especially clear will be how needless any fear you might have ever known was and how if you had only understood better what this was like you would have embraced it gladly, just as you embrace it now.

As you break off your imaginary adventure in dying and return your attention to the here and now, think about the comfort, the assurance of love, the joy you can take into your daily life from the contemplation of your heavenly destiny in Christ Jesus, and how you can dip into this well of hope as often as you wish. Envisioning your own dying can take away any fear you may have of dying, replacing it with a kind of anticipation. By preparing for death you are not hastening its coming, but drawing inspiration and strength to overcome illness and live a rich, productive life. Remember, you have resolved to live to the fullest all the time remaining to you whether you have another four or five decades, or a much shorter time here on earth.

Make an entry in your notebook, recording the new things you have been stimulated to do while you are alive and perhaps describing the effect of imagining the glorious experience of passing through death into *Life*.

Prayers for New Thoughts

Prayer for strength to refuse a death-sentence diagnosis: My Lord and my God, because you said that those who believe in you will never die, I know it must be true. Therefore, I need to believe it with all my spirit, heart, soul, mind, and will. The Spirit of Truth—your own Spirit—is now turning over the broken concrete blocks of my old doubt and ignorance and building new truthful beliefs in me. So with your help, Holy Spirit, I now refuse to accept my diagnosis as a death sentence. Rather, I resolve with your help to make that diagnosis an occasion to refresh, renew, and strengthen my belief in you and your conquest of illness and death.

Prayer to stop imagining that God is against me, and to firmly believe he is on the side of my healing: Because I am a member, by faith, of you, Jesus Christ, I am an heir to the promises made in your Word, which you said cannot be broken. I now, by faith, hear you saying to me personally, "I am the Lord that healeth thee." I am going to stand strong against thoughts that suggest you don't care what happens to me, that you want me to stay ill, or that you hardly ever think about me and my wholeness. I firmly reject those thoughts and others like them, because they make you small instead of the great God that you are. Rather, I join with all the saints and exalt you, and against all lying tongues I insist that you are on the side of my healing because your unbreakable Word says so.

Prayer for my doctor(s), nurses, and other health professionals: I really appreciate my doctor(s), nurses, and other health professionals as gifts from you, dear Father. Thank you for their skills, and for their willingness to help me understand what is going on as my mind and body join together with you and them to fight against disease. I pray for your blessing on the efforts they are making to heal me and other sick people, and I resolve to see them as workers together with you and with me in the struggle toward health. I believe that treatment is a gift from you and that it will be effective against this illness, especially when I combine the efforts of your scientifically trained servants with my progress in replacing lies in my thoughts with the truth.

Prayer of alliance with my body's own health systems: I intend, with your Spirit's aid, to stop thinking of myself and my body as *a disease*, and to fill my mind with the truth that my own hormones and nervous system and immune system as you created them are on the side of my healing. So my own body is working with you and me and my doctors and other health professionals, even now, to overcome this sickness.

Prayer of purpose: You do nothing without a purpose, and I know you have given me a purpose. You have preserved my life to love others and to share Christ, hope, and joy with them. I firmly adopt your purpose for me and declare that I am here to love others and to show your love, no matter what my physical condition is right now.

Praise: I believe—not because I feel but because your Word says—my song is a song of praise. Therefore I will praise you as long as I live, when I feel good and when I feel bad, when I think all is well and when I think nothing is, when I am frustrated and when I am encouraged, when I see no answers and when every wish is fulfilled. All because you dwell in the midst of the praises of your people.

Prayer for God's will: Nothing is higher or better than your will, because you want the best for your children. Whatever you are allowing to happen right now, I know you want only the best for me. Since I may not know what is best, I join my will with yours. And wanting your will for me, I pray your own prayer: Your will be done, Father, here in me as it is in heaven.

Good News Keeps Coming

Recently I received another letter from Dr. Dan Fountain, the man whose treatment for AIDS first kindled my interest in the healing power of a healthy mind. Fountain wrote to me about a man named Joseph, who came to the hospital for relief from pains in the chest, epigastric region, joints, and muscles. A chronic fever came and went, and Joseph had no appetite and was losing weight. Other doctors had treated him without seeing improvement. This thirty-eight-year-old man had cared for his eight children since the death of his first wife five years before. Dr. Fountain wrote:

> On examining him, I found an eight-centimeter mass in the left lobe of his liver. There were no other physical findings and all his lab studies were normal. . . . I prescribed vitamins and a protein-rich diet and referred him to our pastoral care service for encouragement and prayer. One week later he returned to the clinic smiling and much improved. When I examined his abdomen I could no longer find a liver mass. I was astonished.

What had happened to work such a dramatic change so rapidly?

Joseph's counselors had gently helped him confront his inner turmoil. He had had a succession of sexual affairs, even a liaison with his second wife's sister. In his frequent bouts of rage Joseph attacked others physically. He had beaten his older sister who later died of her wounds. On another occasion he wounded and cursed a thief who died shortly thereafter. Joseph felt great remorse over these deaths, but even his visits to the graves of these people did not bring solace.

It was coming to know Jesus Christ through his counselors that changed everything. They showed him how the Lamb of God had carried all his sins to the Cross. Joseph learned that Jesus died for him and rose to triumph over evil. He believed this and accepted Christ as his own Savior. Through subsequent prayer and counseling Joseph felt his burden of guilt begin to fall away.

This was the point at which Dr. Fountain performed his second examination of Joseph and found that the liver mass had vanished. Healing of his mind and spirit had strengthened his body to fight against the physical illness. The result for this man was rapid and complete healing.

For you, too, there will be a positive result. Perhaps it will be complete and immediate healing. More likely, you will experience gradual improvement. First, you will experience the deepest kind of healing as your spirit is reseasoned with a fresh, healthy outlook—a kind of spiritual health that nothing in this world can touch. And as your inner man comes to peace and wholeness, the benefits will spill over into strength, health, and wellness in your physical being.

As you continue to practice the program we have begun together, I know that you will discover for yourself many more benefits of the healing power of a healthy mind.